A Net Full of Tails

Tom Greene

Library of Congress Cataloging-in-Publication is available through the Library of Congress.

ISBN-13: 978-0-9849-3690-8 (soft cover)
ISBN-13: 978-0-9849-3691-5 (hard cover)

Production Management by Sandy Dolan
Cover Photo Pat Ford
Cover Production by Kevin Stawieray
Interior Design and Formatting by Dawn Von Strolley Grove

"To my son Marlin,
who inspired me to sit down
and write this book"

Contents

Acknowledgments

This book was long in the making, and a number of individuals contributed to its content—all of whom are customers and/or friends. First, I'd like to thank those resilient souls who read through these chapters in my inner office, and who offered their advice or verified details. There are far too many of you to include your names, but to those who stayed the course, please accept my gratitude.

Next in line are my fishing buddies—Scott Hitch, Don Caylor and George Copeland—who spent thousands of hours helping me "figure it out." They taught me to love the sport, and together we learned some lasting lessons. Speaking of fishing buddies, who could forget Andy Bean? We spent so much time fishing together that it cost me my marriage. Still, we caught plenty of fish.

Then, I probably wouldn't have written this book were it not for Bill Kane of Boca Tackle. He gave me my very first job, back in 1959. But it wasn't until later that my customers and friends, Joe and Barbara Munson, backed me in a store of my own. Joe went on to fish tournaments in the Keys and Bahamas—many which he won—and he invited me along on a number of occasions.

Thanks to my brother Martin Greene, who worked with me in my store in Deerfield Beach when I first got started—often for starvation wages. He remained with me there for several years, for which I'll be forever grateful. Then, my brother, Russell played a pivotal role, by convincing my mother that my midnight jaunts were simply a cure for snook fishing fever. I was allowed to stay out later than my sisters who dated—an anomaly that Mother never quite understood. Meanwhile, my little sister Nancy deserves credit for encouraging me to write for the past 25 years. Thanks, in fact, to all my siblings—as well as my mother and father—for offering their unwavering support.

I also wish to thank my employees—both past and present—for helping me build a successful business. It bought me the time to work on these stories.

My special thanks to Susan Gillis, curator at the Boca Historical Society, whose impeccable research and attention to detail kept this project going when the going got tough. Susan came up with some incredible images.

Thanks, in addition, to Mike Echols, both in critiquing *A Net Full of Tails* and with my tackle collecting. Were it not for him, Bobby Nicholson and Jimmy Duncan, I'd still be a closet collector. Help, however, comes in many forms.

Take my good friend, Mark Sosin, who wrote the foreword and who offered this piece of advice: "Want more fish? Then, see things the way they do." I've never questioned those words of wisdom that define my outlook today.

Speaking of words, it was Steve Kantner who listened to my ramblings for endless hours before translating them into the writ that follows. He remained undaunted throughout the process. If there's anyone else I've unwittingly forgotten, I hope they keep one thing in mind:

Someone will eventually write on my tombstone:

"Don't brag to me today about how good you are; tell me next year what you learned in the interim."

That's the spirit in which I offer these "tails."

—TG

Foreword

More than 30 years have slipped by since I first met Tommy Greene. He impressed me then with his incredible knowledge of fishing tackle and techniques and he continues to amaze me every time I listen to him. We've fished together off distant shores such as Costa Rica and Venezuela for everything from marlin to roosterfish and we've chased tarpon and snook at our doorstep. And, he's been my guest on a number of television shows focusing on education and information.

Tommy pursues fish with a competitive passion. Watching him in action quickly convinces any onlooker or fishing partner of his remarkable skill with rod and reel and his total understanding of the species he seeks. Said simply, he's one of the best fishermen I know.

Customers who walk into Custom Rod and Reel, Tommy's heavily stocked tackle shop in Lighthouse Point, Florida, are regaled with fishing stories mixed in with educational sessions on how and where to catch a particular species or the gear to use. It's fascinating to hear him share the latest information on what's biting, the bait or lures to use, the hotspots, and anything else an angler needs to know.

Fishing was serious business for Tommy since boyhood. He

had to help feed his family with the fish he caught after school and he also needed to earn money. As a teenager, his first job was in a tackle shop and he learned the business starting with the most menial tasks. It became part of his life and he never strayed from this calling, often working seven days a week once he opened his own store.

A Net Full of Tails captures an assortment of fascinating fishing stories from the days when Tommy rode his bicycle to the fishing spot through a series of adventures enjoyed over many years. Each chapter boasts more than one tale of memorable experiences. Once you start reading this book, it's difficult to put down. You just want to read one more story then the next and the next. Tommy Greene's *A Net Full of Tails* makes fishing come alive and will remind you of some of your own adventures. It's a book that deserves a place in your library.

Mark Sosin
Boca Raton, Florida

Introduction

Fishing, and the fishing business, has been my life since my family moved here in the 1950's. By age 11, I had an after school job—can you believe it?—at a tackle shop. While the other kids were busy playing ball, I was hunting big fish and hanging-out with fish folk. At least, it taught me to tie a few better knots.

I didn't take school for granted. But the time I spent on piers and bridges—and later, in the cockpits of sport fishing yachts—was a lot more fun than study hall. As the years went by, my realm expanded to include all of South Florida, the Keys, and the Bahamas, and ultimately, Cuba, Mexico, Central and South America, as well as "The Land Down-Under."

I collected stories wherever I fished, all which I hope to tell someday. While fish were caught and lessons learned, I enjoyed the tutelage of some true angling legends. Plus, I always received the support of my family. While I got to fish in some wonderful places, it was always with interesting people. For all the above, I'll be forever grateful.

I eventually acquired a shop of my own, which is presently located in Lighthouse Point. While I've met some terrific folks in my travels, and built a successful business, one goal I was never able to achieve was recording my experiences for the sake of posterity. I've seen countless wonders—call it history being made—much of it here at home. But although I'd been lucky and been there, I'd never put any of it down on paper. That's where Steve Kantner came in.

An outdoor writer with a solid reputation, Steve brought his talent to this particular project—proficiency in the types of fishing I've done: As he likes to put it: "Tom and I practically grew-up together, 30 miles apart."

Steve had experienced the same things I had. We shared almost identical backgrounds, and spoke in similar jargon—a prerequisite for compiling this collection of "tails." So I sat down with Steve for the past year-and-a-half, and recounted these stories word for word—some which he'd already heard. Whenever we had to, we researched material in order to provide the most-accurate account, which he then transformed into the writ that follows.

I sincerely hope you enjoy these "fish tails," and that they bring back memories of adventures of your own. If you're the least bit put-off by some of the photos I've included, please keep one thing in mind: We fished primarily to feed our families and none of the fish we caught were ever wasted.

Tom Greene
Lighthouse Point, Florida
September 24, 2011

1

Black Saturday

"As the object kept closing, the fin grew taller."

Photo by Pat Ford.

Ever wonder how it feels?

Sport fishing is a blood sport, pure and simple, and no amount of sanitizing can erase the truth. Using buggy-whip tackle may help cover the stain, but even catch-and-release tactics only mitigate its impact. Fish don't read scripts; they can't predict outcomes, or know ahead of time whether they'll survive these ordeals. The same rule applies to whoever hunts them.

This tale starts out early one Saturday morning nearly 20 years ago. Mark, my companion, who was (and still is) a celebrated outdoor "communicator," needed photos of barracudas for a magazine cover. We planned to catch them on fly gear, as per the editor's request. We'd meet Frank, our guide, at Crandon Park Marina on the shores of Biscayne Bay.

Frank knew the Bay well —like the proverbial back of his hand. After exchanging salutations, we hopped aboard, and he pointed his skiff toward some distant islets where barracudas lurked. A 15-mile romp across turquoise waters awakened our senses. While we reveled in the clarity of the morning sky—and the fact that the temperature had remained reasonably tolerable—the tide continued to fall. If it kept on dropping at its present rate, the flats we were skirting would soon be dry.

We eventually arrived at our destination near some tiny mangrove keys. Since waves were breaking on the ocean-side flats, Frank decided to approach from the rear. We crossed some deeper water, where the bottom darkened as forests of horsetails dropped off towards a few scattered patch reefs.

Previously, we'd been skimming over miles of flats until, as if on cue, Frank turned the wheel. Then we started racing through a maze of channels that vanished into nothing as we neared the shoreline. He eased-up on the throttle before killing the motor, while we paused to assess our surroundings. We would know soon enough if those barracudas were "home."

Frank raised the outboard and grabbed his push pole, as the flats skiff slid to a halt. Now all we could hear was the slap of wavelets—the remnants of what had been our wake. The silence, which was total, was eventually broken by the squawks of seabirds—ones that were nesting nearby. I was amused by a needlefish jumping near some sponges that vaguely resembled overturned flower pots. The flats, we could see, were alive and well.

It's hard to imagine such rampant diversity if you haven't seen it in person. I watched sea grasses bend in the current, while a sting ray exploded from ahead of the bow. The mud trail it left joined a trickle of current that exited the Bay through a mangrove cut. As the sun beat down, it warmed our spirits and set the stage for the morning's fishing. It was finally time to pick up a rod.

Mark stepped onto the forward casting deck, while I found a place near the stern. We watched as a jetliner approached Miami International Airport. However, because of its heading and our position at the time, we never heard so much as a sound. What we noticed was the odor of sulfides that bubbled to the surface on this bayside flats. Was it the result of dead mangroves that were slowly decaying? All I could think of was rotten eggs. But what did it matter on this glorious day?

The barracudas, we discovered, were hungry and eager. We landed several four-footers—all on flies, just like the assignment called for. I slipped over the side at Mark's request, to hold them up for the camera. It's not the kind of thing I enjoy, since the unfortunate consequence of getting perfect photos is that frequently the subject doesn't survive. We placed two of them back in the live-well, in hopes that they might revive.

With our mission accomplished, we paused for a break. I remember drinking water that had gotten so cold that it made my teeth crack when I attempted to sip it. I was covered with sweat and mud by that time, so I welcomed the icy draft.

Frank suggested we try for bonefish—something that required a run back towards Key Biscayne. He had an afternoon charter that he'd meet at the dock, but for now he had time to kill. I looked forward to the prospect of fishing the flats, as well as the breeze we'd feel while moving. The Miami skyline loomed to our left, as Frank pointed the skiff to the north.

It only took a few minutes to make the run, and not much

longer to find the fish. Since the tide was too low for poling the skiff, Frank dropped anchor before starting to chum by tossing out bits of shrimp. The place where we anchored was known as "Stiltsville"—an appropriate description for homes built on pilings. Just imagine a sea of houses, all up on stilts and equipped with docks.

The channels that surround this seagoing subdivision are major gateways to Biscayne Bay. Meanwhile, it didn't take long, as the tide kept falling, until the skiff was hard aground. That inconvenience, however, didn't affect the fishing, which was about to turn-on in earnest.

Once they smelled the shrimp, the bonefish came running. After which we were constantly fighting fish—Mark with his fly rod and I with my bait caster. These fish were large, like most Biscayne "bones" are, and as an additional bonus, we caught jacks and snappers. It was one of those days when it all comes together.

Our reverie was eventually interrupted when Frank opened the live-well and we smelled dead barracuda. The two we'd saved from before had died. Frank tossed both of them overboard, away from our chum slick, each in opposite directions—one off the bow and one off the stern. The stench remained for several more minutes before dispersing in the gentle breeze.

We'd all been busy doing various tasks, not the least of them reeling-in fish. However, now we were victims of that cloying lethargy that conspires with the sun to loosen tight muscles. We were just dozing-off when it caught our eye.

I can't say for sure who saw it first, or recall their initial reaction. What I do remember was someone joking that an "unidentified object" was headed our way. Whatever it was had appeared down-tide and seemed to be moving in our direction. It was accompanied by a flock of seagulls. At this point, no one speculated about the object's identity.

This was, after all, Biscayne Bay—a contemporary Shangri-La, where dreams come true. Was it a submersible craft manned (so-to-speak) by bikini-clad maidens? Or was the University of Miami's Rosenthiel School, which is located around the corner, conducting some type of undersea research? Plenty of outfits had mini-subs, but what was one doing on a bonefish flat?

The object kept getting closer.

At first, all we saw was its wake, as it pushed the water aside with its bulk. Then at 600 yards, something broke the surface, which caused each of us to pay much closer attention. Frank thought he recognized the tip of a fin.

As the object kept closing, the fin grew taller. Three feet or more were completely exposed. In fact, eventually, it started to flop. Could this thing be what we hoped it wasn't?

At 500 yards, we could make out the shape of a bulldozer-like object plowing towards us. Meanwhile, whatever it was refused to veer from its original course. If this was truly a shark, it was the stuff of nightmares.

That's when I recalled a tale from my youth, back in the days when I fished the ocean piers. There was talk of a monster hammerhead that no one could land, regardless of how heavy their tackle. Supposedly, it stripped a series of reels in quick succession. The way I was told, the shark was invincible —a metaphor for the powers of darkness. Did I forget to mention that the shark was black, and that it had a head maybe four feet wide? It's not a story that a kid soon forgets. That's what was going through my head as the juggernaut approached.

By now, the creature was churning-up mud. The mud trail, which must have measured 20 feet across, drifted out to sea with the last of the tide. Was it marking the path to oblivion? This was a hair-raising prospect if ever there was one? Could it be the same hammerhead that had flashed through my memory? Some creatures, I heard, refuse to stop growing.

This species has been known to attack human beings. However, it's their bulldog tenacity that makes them unique in the world of undersea predators. Anyone who's seen it knows what I mean.

Our conversation faltered as the creature got closer. Although we had previously felt safe in the skiff, we were beginning to wonder.

400 yards and closing. Now its tail started lashing the surface. Yet all the while its course never veered.

A large enough hammerhead will attack a full-grown tarpon and tear it to shreds within seconds. Plus, anglers I know of had their boats attacked. While all survived to tell the story, in every instance, the sharks weren't this large.

I'd been watching water skiers in a nearby channel, and marveling at their antics as they jumped boat wakes. They had no idea of the drama that was unfolding a few hundred yards away. With just 300 yards between us and the creature, the taste of pennies now filled my mouth.

Some 200 yards out, the shark ran aground, but that failed to deter its progress. It kept on moving by sheer strength of will, having found a way to force oxygen through its gills, on a flat that was practically devoid of water. Apparently it was digging what we called a "wheel ditch"—one deep enough to float its bulk—while we remained stuck in the marl.

In effect, we were now "sitting ducks." As the shark kept coming, our mood darkened.

The drama had lost its allure. The air, I noticed, was suddenly stifling. Not only did I find it harder to breathe, I had begun to consider the unthinkable. What if the shark actually attacked the skiff and tore-off a piece of the transom? Uncertain of the outcome, we gathered up our tackle and stood closer together in the middle of the skiff.

Time stood still as the shark made its final approach. Meanwhile, all we could do was hold our breath.

At 50 yards out, you could smell the fear that by now had filled the cockpit. Then all at once, the shark picked-up speed until suddenly, it was there—directly alongside us. There was no rolling eye, like with Ahab's whale; nor any sign of higher cognition. Only malevolence incarnate with an anvil head, and a limbic brain to guide its movements.

The shark was half-again as long as the skiff, which measured 17 feet in length overall. Its movements were those of a snake.

I was staring at a creature from the depths of the sea that redefined the meaning of fear. At one point, the monster passed so close that its wake rocked us back and forth. We were much too frightened to comment.

Hammerhead sharks possess elaborate homing mechanisms, as this one was proving while it swam in circles—like a matador turning to face the bull. Then in blind-eyed urgency, it discovered a barracuda that was lying there on the bottom. Which then disappeared in a single gulp.

As quickly as the shark had materialized, it turned and started to swim off the flat on the same path it followed when it made its approach. A full minute passed before anyone breathed.

What I couldn't shake was the image of that head, swinging from side to side. The mouth beneath it could have chewed through the hull and spit out fiberglass splinters like tooth picks, before turning its attention to what was inside. We kept holding our breath while it continued seaward. Then, finally we were able to talk.

We could see the shark's tail still churning up mud, as it exited the flat. Meanwhile, people on sail boats in a nearby channel were preparing to take a swim. But why upset them now that the threat was gone? We had managed to survive the ordeal.

All we could do was stand and stare, while the monster retraced its path to the deep. The largest shark we had ever seen had put us in fear for our lives—and whether or not those fears were grounded, they were certainly real to us.

What if those barracudas had remained in the well? Or what

about the snappers that were alive and flopping? The hair stood up on the back of my neck when I paused to consider the possibilities.

Then the impossible happened.

The shark, which had traveled several hundred yards at this point, halted abruptly before turning around.

The breath felt trapped in my lungs.

It was headed back with a vengeance. Was it the scent of cuda, or the skiff itself? If that first approach was a cause for alarm, then this one would be horrific. We braced for another onslaught.

By now, the tide had started to rise, while the current kept moving towards the ocean depths. It's an anomaly that few anglers are aware of, this separation of phase and direction—essentially of depth and flow. Sharks, however, use it to their advantage in order to hunt the flats.

The shark closed-in quicker than it had before, veering to one side as it passed the bow, before turning and beginning to search again. Imagine this monster just beyond your gunwales. We prayed it would find that second cuda before deciding to change the menu.

What else to do but look on in horror? While the shark's every movement remains etched in my mind, I found its resolve the most-disquieting. In the simplest of terms, it wouldn't give-up the chase until, in a mud-strewn finale, it found that cuda. Having apparently missed it on the initial approach, it picked-up the scent while departing the flat—which accounted for the final turnaround.

We all remained silent as it swam out to sea, and the only sounds were those of the gulls. Mark's fingers were frozen by this vision of terror. It was only after the spell was finally broken that he responded with a few last-minute clicks. When the photos were developed, all they showed was the fin disappearing beneath the waves. Two cameras hung around his neck at the time.

The tide continued to flood the flat, as Frank pulled the anchor and we stowed our gear. I recall that no one spoke on the way to the dock. A crisis averted affects everyone differently, but its collective impact was surprisingly similar. While I seldom speak of that trip anymore, I remember the day when the hunters were hunted.

Plus, I consider myself lucky to have been released without bloodshed.

2

The Longest Night

"Some have names that evoke the past, like
Tea Table Relief and Indian Key Viaduct."

Looking for a life lesson? You'll find it here.

Forget about fiberglass yachts and glistening fillets: sport fishing is all about heart. While fishermen run the gamut from felons to kings, the most memorable often appear quite ordinary—if you're willing to overlook a few minor details. Take my good friend, Harvey:

He was the biggest man I've ever known. At six-foot-eight, and nearly 350 pounds, he was born to the position of All-State fullback: a distinction he retained throughout his high school career. But what outweighed his stature was his competitive nature, which permeated everything he did.

A giant of a man with a heart of gold, he succeeded where others failed: mostly by refusing to say "I can't." He was gentle-natured unless deliberately provoked, and as loyal a buddy as I could have ever wanted. I'm proud to have called him my friend.

The tarpon, you may have heard, is a character, too, and born to a single purpose: that of staying alive. While the majority of tarpon are smaller than Harvey, occasional exceptions are known to exist. When it comes down to grit, the two run neck-in-neck, which leads to a singular tale:

Picture the bridges of the Overseas Highway, as they follow the sunset into the Gulf of Mexico. Then envision them prior to 1970, before millionaire developers commercialized the Keys. If U.S.1 wasn't completely deserted, it was far less-traveled than it is today. While Keys residents stayed pleasantly out-of-touch, they regaled in their anonymity. Among the "locals" were schools of tarpon—only a fraction of which ply those waters today.

Once you reach Islamorada—maybe halfway between Key West and Miami—the spans get longer and the channels, deeper. That's where the largest tarpon gather, starting in May, around the time when the Poincianas bloom. Witness the latter event and you'll be regaled by Nature. But to understand tarpon, you first undergo pain.

Because it's only after your endurance is tested, that you finally decide to put it all on the line. But that's what it takes, maybe once in a lifetime, when it all boils down to not giving up. Call it competition, or the essence of sport, but I can't help thinking of torture. So how did I reach such a macabre conclusion?

At one time, my friends and I fished those bridges—for tarpon at night, during May and June. From the time I purchased my very first car, I'd grab-up my gear on Friday night and dash for the door when the boss closed the shop. We'd take Florida's Turnpike to Homestead, then hit U.S. 1 and keep heading south. Who can forget the heat and mosquitoes?

I can picture that all-night tackle shop that was south of Homestead on U.S.1: We'd stop there for sodas and snacks, in hopes of beating the heat. I'm reminded that it smelled like mullet and shrimp, and the boxes of frozen squid. We eschewed all those options in favor of lures—specifically, the Creek Chub Pikie—because of the whims of our quarry. We had miles to go before we'd fish, and it seemed we were always chasing the tide. Keys bridges, in those days, were a study in stone, or a history lesson might be a better term.

Some have names that evoke the past, like Tea Table Relief and Indian Key Viaduct. Whale Harbor and Snake Creek sound more romantic, although I don't recall seeing whales or snakes. One bridge in particular, Channel Number 5, was a perennial favorite of ours for tarpon. Two contiguous spans, Channel 2 and Long Key Viaduct, were also contenders, depending on the tide.

To be successful at bridge fishing you need to know the following rule: It's the tide that makes all the difference. Here's how it works in the Keys:

Celestial forces create powerful currents that surge back and forth through the concrete arches. The current, in turn, can work for or against you, depending on how much forage it carries, as well as your ability to handle your tackle. Tides are cafeterias to the legions of tarpon, which spend most of their lives searching for food. Meanwhile, getting back to Channel 5. . . .

At the start of the ebb, the tarpon would gather on the up-current side and wait for sunset. Before the fireworks began in earnest. Billions of gallons of seawater carried all types of prey through the span. Since the tarpon, for the most part, were the giants of their species, and since the carnage was unimaginable by today's standards, you had to have seen it to imagine the ruckus.

Mullet and ballyhoo, along with countless invertebrates, were swept towards the waiting shadow line. There weren't any lights per se: only the moon and stars cast the faintest of shadows. Yet the killing zone was well-defined, and while diaphanous organisms glowed deep in the current, billows of green erupted on top. The cacophony would escalate to a deafening pitch, as it echoed between the caissons. It was like listening to a symphony from Hell.

There's something primal about fishing for monsters, especially when you're practically alone at the time. But like I said, you had to be there. Perhaps a word about tackle would be in order?

I relied on a heavy fiberglass bridge rod, to which I'd bolted a 4/0 reel that I'd customized for casting big plugs. I didn't waste time with gossamer lines, choosing instead to go all-out: With 50-pound test or better, I enjoyed equal footing with the tarpon I hooked. Or so I liked to believe. My rod, I might add, was 10 feet long. That meant if I lost my balance, or leaned too far forward, the mechanical advantage could send me flying. That's something I tried to avoid.

The rules of engagement were simple: Cast a 6900 series Pikie at an angle to the bridge; then, reel it back faster than the current. Even today, Pikies enjoy a reputation, but that's another story.

Those hardwood lures sported three sets of trebles that could probably hoist a steer. During a particularly memorable, previous outing, I landed a tarpon over 200 pounds. We weighed it at Bud and Mary's, in the days before catch and release. The fish hit a Pikie.

Meanwhile, the tarpon that inspired this particular story hit at precisely 12:43 A.M.—something I know from Harvey's watch. In the beginning, it behaved like most of them do, while Harvey stood ready with the bridge gaff. Then everything changed in a heartbeat. Remember me mentioning the connection between fishing and "heart?" The following will explain it in additional detail:

Harvey stayed alongside me for most of the night, despite a plaster cast that hampered his movements. It covered his foot all the way to his ankle, yet I doubt if he felt he was crippled. He had broken his toes while installing a roof, when he landed feet-first on a two-by-four. But that didn't stop him from finishing the job. Like always, he wanted to do his part, and no one loved fishing more than he did. He knew that I'd do the same for him, but getting back to that tarpon:

I realized early-on that something was different when I failed to turn its head right away. The strike had felt like I'd hit a wall, except that this wall kept moving without breaking the surface. Most 100-pounders jump when you hook them, then two minutes later, they're flat on their sides. But this one just powered into the current until suddenly, my line went slack.

I realized that it had reversed its course, and that it was probably headed back to the bridge. So I took off in its general direction, while running and reeling as fast as I could. My pulse by this time was pounding wildly, but everything else was deathly still. Except for my breath, which was coming in gasps. I started to taste those sodas again, and the bridge all around me looked dark and forbidding. At this point, I still hadn't run very far.

The standard response at times like these is to quickly prepare for the worst. Say your fish decides to charge the bridge and barrel full-tilt out the other side. Because of the angle, and the abrasive concrete, this invariably results in broken tackle. Unless you pull-off a trick we learned.

The tarpon did what I hoped it wouldn't, while ripping-off line in the process. So I yelled to Harvey to take the bridge gaff and lower it down on the opposite side. He stumbled across the high-way, and managed to lower the gaff in record time. If everything gelled, he'd snag my line and, soon enough, he'd be able to grab it. So I could drop my rod underneath the bridge, and continue fighting on the other side.

But while the seconds passed and the tension mounted, he couldn't find my line—by dragging the gaff hook between the caissons, where it should have been. Now, all I could do was take my reel out of gear.

Backing-off on the tension would change the angle of pull, while allowing the tarpon to run away from the bridge, thereby allowing the line to lift. Once Harvey could snag it and grab the mono, I'd throw my reel into gear again and drop the outfit overboard.

Then I'd run over to Harvey, after letting go, and help him lift it over the opposite railing. If we worked together, it would barely get wet. Then I'd be tight to the fish on the other side, and in a position where the odds were more in my favor. I caution any neophytes to avoid this stunt.

But Harvey still couldn't locate the line, after repeatedly dragging the gaff back and forth. I watched him stumble on his injured foot, while the line on my spool continued to dwindle. Nothing made sense anymore at this point. Where was my line, if not where he'd looked?

All I could think of was that the fish had run under and circled a caisson before swimming out again. Was the tarpon continuing on its former course? In response to my yelling, and with no time to lose, Harvey hobbled back to my side of the bridge.

That's where, in less than a minute, he snagged the line in the only other place he could possibly find it. The fish had indeed circled the caisson, leaving us to solve the riddle. Harvey eventually got hold of the mono, before I tightened my drag and dropped the rod. While he stood there holding his breath, we both started pulling until I was able to grab it, and take-off running down the bridge again.

I was back on track, but so was the fish, which kept heading toward the draw span. That spelled trouble under normal conditions, but all I could do was pull and pray.

The battle dragged us for miles from where we started—me with the fish and Harvey with his cast. Since there weren't any catwalks on this particular bridge—only inches of concrete and steel I-beam railing—we were in constant danger from passing traffic. Surrounded by darkness, and starting to weaken, my thoughts were beginning to blur:

"Truck's getting closer, I can see the sparks; 18-wheeler in the southbound lane. Mirrors touched the guardrail; driver must be dozing. I warn Harvey to scramble to the opposite side. Nothing between us and the abyss below."

So once again, I loosen my drag, and straddle the railing while clutching my rod. Then, this idiot honks, like it's all my fault, and as quickly as they appeared, the lights vanish. Bathed in darkness, I swing onto the tarmac, and take off running and reeling again. The fish, I can tell, is still heading east. If only my rod were two feet shorter.

It's already been at least two hours; no time to let-up or weaken. Thumb's bleeding badly: nicked to the bone. Cuts and scrapes all burning at once. The taste in my mouth is of ice-cold metal, and there's bile in the back of my throat. But the ordeal continues on into the night.

Ribs must be bruised; it hurts to breathe. Rod butt is locked in my armpit. "Fish, please slow down and roll on your side, before I lose my grip." Legs are shaking, arms are cramped. Harvey tells me it's been three hours. He's struggling to keep the pace. I mumble something before the fish turns around starts swimming towards the beach. Which at Channel 5 is a rocky buttress. Did I mention that the tide had changed?

So it's retrace my steps, and keep-up the pressure, although nothing I do seems to phase this behemoth. How big could it possibly be?

Miles to shore, with me on a tether: Or better, a mono leash, at the end of a 10-foot lever—one capable of exerting tremendous mechanical advantage. I can't take much more, if she doesn't quit soon. Then I look at Harvey, who's there at my side again.

Limping and stumbling, he pauses momentarily and spits these words at my face: "Don't even think about it, you son-of-a bitch."

And so we keep marching to the end of the bridge.

For a change I think I'm making some progress, with the fish near the bulkhead and me, off the bridge. Harvey has to struggle when we get to the rocks, but he claws his way along the treacherous slope. We eventually work our way to a canal and a seawall, where for the first time we see the fish.

I can barely believe my eyes.

There, in slack current and barely upright, swims the largest tarpon I'd ever seen. And there in her jaw hangs the Pikie, with the lead hook hung in her gill plate. A few more cranks and I'll lift her nose; then finally the victory is mine. But some things simply aren't meant to be.

Due to the angle between me and that plug, I'm unable to keep her nose on top. So on fourth and ten, she stages a rally and decides to run with the ball. My drag barely slips, but that's enough. Then, suddenly she's swimming towards the bridge again. I stumble towards the rocks with Harvey in tow.

For the past four hours, he'd been carrying the bridge gaff: a heavy affair made for lifting big fish. In the event I'd held her, we'd have gaffed that tarpon, and dragged her to the nearest scale. She was just too big to release, at a time in our lives when bigger meant better. Somehow, I lost Harvey in those final moments when the world around me spun out of control.

The final hour seems more like a dream. The tarpon, I remember, picked-up speed, fueled by a second wind. While the battering continued, I re-traced my steps towards the draw span, and the fenders that lay beneath it.

But this time she managed to make it, and with a final effort, she ran through the pilings and cut my line in the process. I dropped to my knees, exhausted, my body and mind too numb to feel. I knew neither relief nor disappointment, only the reality that the fish was gone.

Eventually, my surroundings came back into focus, as a late-night delivery truck passed by in the darkness. I finally stood up on my feet. My face, I guessed, looked flushed and haggard. It was a long way back to where this had all begun. That's especially true when you're doing the limping. My throat was parched, but I kept on moving, while I pondered the enormity of what had just happened.

Of all God's sea-going creatures, I'd just been trounced by the gamest, and one of the largest to boot. I remembered that the largest tarpon on record, netted by a commercial fisherman in Hillsboro Inlet, weighed 350 pounds. It measured eight feet-something in length. The one I'd lost was at least that large. The IGFA All-Tackle World Record remains quite a bit less.

Just then, I saw Harvey stumbling towards me in the moon-light. He was dragging that bridge gaff, like he had all along. His clothes looked tattered from what I could tell, and I could only imagine what had become of his cast. When he saw me coming, he knew what had happened. A minute or two later, when he got within earshot, I heard him yell these prophetic words:

"I knew you'd never land her. The two of us together didn't stand a chance."

That summed it up in a way that I couldn't. There's nothing to do at a time like this, but share the experience with a kindred spirit. Harvey had written the book on competition, but he always insisted on playing fair. I hope my answer reflected that fact:

"I'm happy to think she made it, because she definitely kicked my ass."

We stumbled back towards the shore together, too weary to face the dawn. The mosquitoes, we noticed, were winding down, and every so often a car would pass. It would be weeks until all our wounds healed.

It's been 40 years since that incredible night that I still remember as if it was yesterday. That fish, like Harvey, showed indomitable courage, and both of them rank as my heroes.

Like I said before, I hope she made it. Meanwhile, Harvey died while watching TV—yelling at his set during Monday Night Football. I think of them both all the time, especially while I'm watching those games myself.

I always figured that football, like fishing, is all about heart.

3

A Man's Time

"Tom Greene with a limit of snook from the bridges."

Photo courtesy of Tom Greene.

Some bridges are easier to cross than others

I figure you can get away with just about anything—if you're willing not to lie about it or make false claims. I make my living selling fishing tackle, and I never pretend to do anything else. I am, however, a pretty fair snook fisherman, which led to an offer I couldn't refuse.

Commerce, after all, is about priorities and that means paying the bills. So like most working stiffs, I get up too early and race off to work—a tackle shop. While the owners and locations have changed in the past, the routine remains the same: Long days in a row with little time off, except when we close and maybe on Sundays. So I've learned to enjoy my leisure.

Now, the following took place when I was younger, but if the characters have changed, the moral has not. It's about putting a price on my leisure time, along with camaraderie and the joys of fishing:

Well, I'm standing behind the counter when the telephone in front of me rings. I don't recognize the caller, but he asks for me by name. Here, as I recall, is how it went:

"Tom Greene?"

"Yes?"

"This is Mr. So-and-So. How's the snook fishing?"

Snook, I thought. Hmmm.

"Pretty good, sir: Plenty of fish at the inlets, and they're knocking 'em dead at the piers. Plus, the Palm Beach bridges are producing consistently."

Then he proceeds to catch me off-guard:

"I'd like to charter you for three days of fishing. We'd really like to catch a big one."

Unsure of what to say, I let the caller continue:

"I hear that snook are great eating?"

Still at a loss, I agree. Who should know any better, after feeding it to my family since I was a boy? My father was blind and my mother, ill, so we all relied on snook. Tasty, indeed; as good as it gets. But would opportunity replace necessity? The caller continued his pitch:

"A business associate and I will be traveling to Palm Beach on Friday. We'll find a hotel. Meanwhile, we'd like to book you for the weekend"

The following may sound a bit garbled, but it's how I remember my answer:

"Mr. So-and-So, I don't 'guide' per se. However, I'll give you the names of captains who do. They'll be happy to accommodate you, I'm sure. These guys get anywhere from $200 to $250 per day, depending on where they fish."

"But you're the best, and that's what we want."

"(Embarrassed) I answer:

"Some folks say that, but I also run a tackle business that takes-up all of my time. So any time off is strictly my own."

His turn now:

"All we want is to catch big snook. We recently returned from Costa Rica, and all we got there were a couple of dinks. Everyone tells us that you're the best."

"I probably am," said I, without blushing.

"That's a bit cocky," he said in return. To which I replied: "The way I recall, you called me."

"You're right, I did," he answered. "But of course, we intend to pay you."

"I assumed that already," I instinctively responded. "But I doubt if you're willing to pay what I'd ask for."

"Try me," he said in return.

Suddenly, my thoughts were in free-fall. I'd been putting in extra time for several months running, with tournament season and Bahamas crossings—plus, fishing late at night before catching a catnap and crawling into work. So I needed rest like a runner needs water. Then I looked out the window at my tattered El Camino and thought: 'Maybe I'll give it a try?'

So I told the caller a thousand bucks a day, to which he replied: "Done."

I nearly fell off the stool.

I arranged to meet them at Palm Beach International and drive them to wherever they'd decided to stay. A few hours later, we'd meet up again, and that's when I'd take them fishing. They were arriving at 7:00 P.M. on a private aircraft, but I figured I'd find them once they told me the concourse. The only other information I knew at that point was that both of them hailed from the Midwest.

I suggested they plan on grabbing some dinner before I returned and picked them up. We'd need time to catch live bait prior to the tide change. In snook fishing, both make a difference. So at that moment I became Tom Greene, guide.

I must have been late, because at the airport they were wearing that look—the one big shots get when they're kept waiting. Well, I'm happy to report that their ire subsided, once I explained I'd been held-up in traffic. Those were the days before the Interstate highway.

Their hotel turned out to be the Breakers, which, if you didn't know, is on Palm Beach Island—not far from where I intended to fish. The Breakers is ritzy, if you'll forgive the pun, and situated on 140 secluded acres. At this point, we were still at the airport.

When I went to toss their bags into the El Camino, I noticed they were wearing fly fishing vests, which here in South Florida, is the sign of a tyro. They looked like they'd stepped from a Herter's catalog. Plus, both wore hats with lamb's wool bands into which they'd slipped several well-worn wet flies. They could have been the directors of Chase Manhattan, but they looked like Lewis and Clark. In silence, I bit my lip.

When we first pulled-up in front of the Breakers, the doorman was biting his, too. Was it my El Camino with its rusty side panels, my ten-foot bridge rods, or my customers' outfits? I'll bet he was wondering if Addison Mizner (the architect who designed this and other Palm Beach landmarks) was rolling in his grave. I'd prefer to think that Mizner was laughing when I dropped them off without further ado.

I drove off in the direction of Lake Worth Lagoon and beyond it, the lights of West Palm Beach. That's where guys like me can get lost in the crowd, a mile from all the heiresses and movie stars. But it's also where I could grab a cheeseburger, and plan my strategy for what lay ahead.

Since the lagoon and the Breakers weren't far apart, I reached the bridge in record time. The draw span was up when I arrived at the channel, giving me ample time to consider the evening. I glanced out my window at the glowing neon, and the expanse of water that lay to the north. While tiny wavelets danced in the moonlight, the tide continued to rise.

I returned to the Breakers two hours later with my aerator buzzing like a punch-drunk locust. I'd filled the live well with water from the lagoon, a detail better left to guides. Several monofilament cast nets were arranged on my truck bed, where I'd also pinioned a wooden dolly. When my clients stepped from the hotel's ornate lobby, they looked primed and ready to go.

The time had come to wake-up and fish, since snook are notorious night owls. Evening Number One would begin on a premise that I needed to explain from the start:

"First, we catch live bait. Then it's back to the bridge, where you'll catch the snook."

All I received in return was a stare, as if I'd stunned my clients instead of informing them. "Bridge, you say? Catch our own bait? Where's the boat?"

I figured this could turn into a really long night, unless they got something straight. So here's what I said in response:

"You heard me right. That's how we do it. Forget about boats; we catch snook from bridges."

Their lack of confidence unnerved me a bit, since I needed their trust to make the plan work. So I immediately attempted to squelch any doubts.

"Weren't you the guys who demanded the best? Well, that's what you're about to get. Catching the live bait is a part of it. Without it, you can't do the rest."

It appeared I had made my point. Perhaps additional background may be in order?

Snook in the lagoon feed on sand perch and mullet during summer, which is when these events took place. And the way we catch both is by throwing a cast net. Bemused at the prospect, they climbed aboard. Then it was off to the Earmine River.

Leaving the Palm Beach Island may cause culture shock. Get to the mainland, specifically Federal Highway, and you're close to the worst part of town. The civility you see in your rear-view mirror seems light-years away—amid the pawn shops, bars and assorted strip joints. But downtown West Palm was like that back then, when the dregs of humanity wandered the streets. I took a right on Federal and headed north.

To the right stretched the Port of Palm Beach—a steam-spitting monster with the soul of a robot. Then, next came Riviera Beach, where the name and lifestyle didn't quite fit: hardly the place to be changing a tire.

If you kept on going, you'd come to a stretch where the life of your wallet wasn't measured in minutes. Then, the urban sprawl begins to recede, and you cross a waterway that resembles a canal. That's the Earmine River.

I pulled off Federal in total darkness, and parked near a vacant bank, before giving each of my charges a five gallon bucket, along with a towel and a lecture on mullet. I'd be the one with the cast net. With any luck, we could work together.

We stumbled down the embankment onto slime-covered rocks, at which time I searched the shallows. Not long afterwards, I discovered a disturbance that turned out to be mullet headed our way.

I unfurled my cast net and waited, while both men stood behind me in awe. After telling them both to remain completely still, I lifted my arms and got ready to throw. The night, I assured them, would be filled with wonders.

When I released the net, it opened completely, causing the two to recoil. Then, when I tucked the drawstrings, they both started hollering like kids on the last day of school. Who could miss all that splashing?

The net had trapped a dozen baits. While my customers stood with their half-filled buckets, I emptied the net into each. Mullet were jumping out everywhere, and both men laughed as they bent to retrieve them. After hurriedly rushing them back to the truck, they dumped the baits into my live well.

We'd gotten an auspicious start. Already, we smelled like fish. It all gets easier once you break the ice.

We repeated the routine a time or two, before loading our gear and hitting the road. Our live well full, and with time a-wasting, we needed to catch the high falling tide. So it was back to Flagler Bridge and Palm Beach Island.

Several spans connect Palm Beach to the mainland, but I planned on fishing that one near the Breakers—an anomaly that baffled my charges. But that's where the snook had been hitting lately. You learn these things when you work in my business. So, essentially, all we did was backtrack. I felt more like a chauffer than a fishing guide.

I explained to both men the importance of tides, which were an hour apart at the different bridges, and the connection between snook and shadow lines. At Flagler that meant the fourth light from shore. I knew the tide had already turned, so I stepped on the gas when the light turned green.

We eventually arrived at the foot of the bridge, where we unloaded my dolly, along with our gear. I referred to the dolly as "Dolly Mullet," a fanciful name for a basic tool, but a friend to those of us who live-bait for snook. Without a supply of fresh bait on hand, fishing slows to a crawl. And a full 50 gallon live well was too heavy to carry. We set the gear beneath a street lamp.

Imagine a world apart. That's how it is on these dimly-lit spans, even after your eyes adjust to the dark. While both the sidewalk and road bask in the glow of street lights, events in the water are never that clear—which puts a premium on observation. I reached in the well for a live bait, while grasping a super-sharp 8/0 hook. But instead of a mullet, I came up with a sand perch, which works just as well and sometimes, better.

I inserted the hook in its vent, while attempting to minimize any unnecessary damage. It's a trick I learned that lets the hook tear free before the snook can eject the bait.

"Ouch!" I thought, but it's not so bad. Plus, the bait survives— if the snook coughs it up. Not to mention that the idea behind it is to cause the bait to swim to where the snook are.

Drop a vent-hooked sand perch from any bridge, and the first thing it does is head for the bottom. That's what I wanted, while I fed out line, before handing the rod to the first of my charges. We were 20 feet from the nearest piling, standing directly beneath the light. Our only company was a halo of bugs, and an occasional car that passed in the night.

We didn't have long to wait. I'd instructed my charges, if they felt a "thump," to drop the rod tip and come-up hard. But that initial strike caught the first guy off-guard, and changed his position on fishing for snook.

All I heard was "I think I've got one," when a snook hooked itself and took off running. A 10-foot bridge rod is a formidable weapon, so when the fish got going, the guy lost his footing— allowing the fish to drag him down the railing.

The line hit some pilings and parted before the snook inflicted any further damage. But the guy who I thought might be the boss now lay bleeding from multiple scrapes. Instead of complaining, he brushed off the grime, and asked to get back in the game.

"Yes," I assured him. But this time I'd know the second his bait acted-up. The bait's swimming motion feels different from a hit, but from 20 feet up, there's some confusion. An unfortunate consequence of fishing a vent-hooked bait is that you can't always tell the two apart. As I reached into the bucket for another bait, he asked to try the rest for himself. So I hooked the bait and handed him the rod.

Thirty seconds later he felt the thump, and without hesitation, hauled back on the rod. The tug-o'-war lasted less than a minute before a 15-pound snook lay stretched out on top. I lowered the rope gaff and hooked his catch, which I hurriedly dragged over the railing. To say he was ecstatic was putting it mildly. And so was with his partner, who was next in line.

Class was finally in session. The lesson would last for the rest of the weekend, while my students honed their skills in the glow of a street light. For what they were paying, they deserved a tutor, and that's what I decided they'd get.

When the tide finally slowed to a trickle, streaks of pink lined the eastern horizon. So we loaded the gear in my El Camino, while savoring the prospect of a hearty breakfast.

Later, while we were eating, both men admitted that they'd had the time of their lives. Their mood had changed, they were much more-relaxed. Although we never discussed what they did for a living, I guessed they were successful, and judging from their pluck, that both had worked for their fortunes. It hardly mattered in the overall scheme. Come Evening Number Two, they'd be "ready to rumble."

They were indeed. After picking them up and arranging our

gear, I took plenty of time showing them the ropes. We retracted our path to the Earmine River, where I started them throwing the cast net. They'd stand on the bank, all draped in mesh, as they gripped the leads in their teeth. They learned early-on how to twist their torsos in order to generate the needed spin.

Their first attempts netted coconuts and palm fronds. But it wasn't long afterwards that they discovered some mullet that were traveling in the company of sand perch.

The net opened wide and they filled the bucket. At that point, I could say that they'd caught their own bait. In spite of the excitement, I couldn't help noticing that they'd exchanged their outfits for department store blue jeans.

Later that night, the bridge came alive with "pops" and splashes that echoed loudly. Each man threw the net over schools of mullet that raced through the span while evading snook. They used those live baits to land half a dozen "line-siders"—their limit, which I'd clean later on.

I performed the honors on the bed of my truck, while explaining the process in detail—how we filleted and skinned these Florida fish. Then I placed the fillets in plastic bags that I buried deep in my ice-filled cooler.

At breakfast, they spoke like seasoned veterans who'd cut their teeth, as well as their forearms, on concrete spans like the one we'd fished. Meanwhile, neither complained about those scrapes and contusions that spoke to the power of 80-pound test. Our waitress, a shapely brunette, asked if we'd been "out fishing."

We explained that we had, before she left with our orders—a

move we awaited with baited breath. After three days of nothing but male companionship, we wanted a better look. That night, we'd meet-up an hour later. It all had to do with the tide.

Night Number Three started out like before, but by this time my charges had valuable experience. They jumped at the chance to net their own bait, and both caught limits of snook—with minimal assistance from yours truly. They'd run up and down, with two rods and a cast net, and wherever a snook "popped," they'd give it a try.

They'd become proficient enough to gaff their own fish—a skill reserved for experienced anglers. So when the first rays of dawn appeared on the horizon, four 20-pounders lay stacked on the sidewalk. Those were the days of four-fish limits, and we hadn't started fishing until well past midnight.

I collected the fillets from our previous outings, which I'd wrapped and stacked in my freezer in Boca. I'd planned to add them to that final night's take, according to prior arrangement. Between the ones they'd just caught, and the fish from before, they had more than 100 pounds of boneless fillets: Clean, white meat fit for a king; the same I fed it to my parents and siblings. Breakfast that morning would be our last.

By now, they'd relaxed even more, although we all drank coffee like it was going out of style. Our waitress asked again if we'd spent the night fishing, and we suggested she look in the truck. It was barely daylight outside the 24-hour restaurant, so several co-workers accompanied her to the lot.

You'd think Moby Dick was there in my cooler, instead of snook carcasses and bags of fillets. In the meantime, one of my clients—the senior of the two, I believe—reached in his pocket and handed me a check. I thanked him politely and tucked it away. Our conversation continued without hesitation, and it wasn't until later that he asked if I'd read it.

I had to admit that I hadn't.

Both men stared like I'd lost my mind. So I reached in my pocket and withdrew the check. I'd expected the full $3,000, but the check was made out for considerably more: $5,000, as a matter of fact.

I had no idea what to say. Until the guy who'd written it broke the silence:

"Look, this was the most fun we've had in some time. It was worth every cent; in fact, we felt, more. But before we go out again with you, use the extra cash to replace your floor boards, so our feet don't drag on the pavement."

I nodded contritely, knowing what they meant. But the best part was yet to come:

His partner and I were waiting outside, while my benefactor used the restroom, when the guy remarks with a chuckle:

"Think it was worth it—I mean, taking us fishing? You could have sold a photo of him running on that bridge to the *National Enquirer* for a helluva lot more—than you made off us."

I didn't know whether he was kidding or not. Until I re-read the name on the check.

4

A Collector of Shiny Things

"Tom, in his office, surrounded by antique tackle."

Like a needle in a haystack

Men are collectors of value and beauty, a procliv-ity they've indulged since the dawn of time. The objects of their attentions range from sports cars to starlets, while mine have remained a bit more-practical (as well as a lot less-expensive). Namely, I specialize in antique fishing tackle (the kind you find stashed in Grandma's attic) that I buy and sell as a sideline. Over the years I've discovered a few "finds," like: 'if collecting isn't a money-maker, then it's still lots of fun.'

It's the kind of business where you try to stay current, and where bad decisions can cost you money. Although failures are common in our volatile economy, rewards in collecting are even further between. Hands-on experience is helpful and thankfully, I'm familiar with most types of tackle. Or so I used to believe.

My initial understanding of what was "out there" came as a result of my very first job. I started working in tackle shops as a kid, and I'm still at it decades later. Back then, you spent ten bucks for a box of wooden Zaragossas, before feeding them to hungry jacks and bluefish. Try that today, and you'd need a hedge fund—meaning that certain collectibles have gotten downright expensive.

Perhaps I'm showing my age? Yet it's hard not to notice that the tackle I'm collecting is the same stuff I fished with a few years back. Just think of the inventions we take for granted, like injection-molding and super-braid lines. What if we had them when we were younger? Knowledge, they say, is exponential. Meanwhile, antique tackle possesses a charm—one that transcends modern marvels. That's the part I can't get past, like a love-sick peasant who falls in love with a queen.

You can smell it all over my office, where most of my collecting takes place. Be it the scent of hardwood, or ancient reel oil, these treasures emit a special perfume. Whether something's worthless, or a work of art, I won't know for sure until I see it up close. And I'm not the only one looking. Most collectibles were produced in small machine shops, although others emerged from full-fledged factories—wherever dreamers out-numbered the accountants.

❖ ❖ ❖

Several older companies, ones bought-out by big corporations, hold reunions for their former employees. These get-togethers, and I occasionally attend one, attract multiple generations of a number of families. All these people worked for the company at one time or another.

Tackle-making was considered a craft, as American as apple pie. Of course, those were the days when workmanship mattered, as is evident from the paint job on a Creek Chub "Pikie," or the sheen on the side plates of an antique reel. Visit an antique tackle show for clarification.

I once met a guy—a full-time collector—who spent his summers traveling the countryside in search of the ultimate "buy." To him, it was all about gaining access: to farmhouses, or wherever folks kept their heirlooms. He rang plenty of doorbells in his quest for junk, but every so often, he'd hit the jackpot.

He must have had the eyes of an eagle, since he knew at a glance if the place held a treasure. If something looked old, he'd make an offer, before producing a thick wad of bills. He'd pay top dollar for some worthless relic, and save the remainder for later. Hard cash, you could say, was his stock in trade, as was his poker face. His goal in life was to make a score, and he knew how to hunt over a baited field.

Say, a farmer just sold him a picture frame—one that had languished in a shed or an attic—for maybe a hundred bucks. Then, for a few dollars more, he'd buy a rod or reel that, unlike the frame, was worth a fortune. People seldom argued with easy money, especially when it arrived with so little warning. So in the end, everyone walked away happy: the perfect denouement to a labor of love.

To him, buying tackle was just the tip of the iceberg. One day all that picking uncovered a treasure: a painting that turned out to be a bona fide Rembrandt. It was valued at over a million dollars. When I asked him what he intended to do with it, he said: "Hang it on my wall." As fate would have it, he was the scion of a wealthy family, who collected primarily for the enjoyment it gave him.

My own addiction took a different route.

A collector buddy, Bobby Nicholson, invited me to join him at a show in West Palm Beach—nearly 30 years ago. That's quite a ways from my usual stomping grounds, but Bob's a friend so I agreed to go. He even offered to give me a ride, a move I'm sure he later regretted. Bob, by the way, is a first-rate angler.

Attend I did, and I really enjoyed it, until it came to the part where Bob started haggling. We were walking along a row of tables where vendors displayed their wares. Like everyone else, Bob was looking for deals.

Try to visualize the Mona Lisa. That's a fair comparison, if you're into collecting, of a frog carved by master craftsman, James Heddon, of Dowagiac, Michigan. Heddon whittled imitations over 100 years ago that still serve as models for surface lures. I doubt if he ever carved more than a dozen, but there on a table, Bob thinks he sees one.

What followed began like a symphony, with opening movements from both sides of the table. The first notes sounded like this:

"Nice plug," Bob muttered in a quiet voice. Then more emphatically: "You think it's an original?" The volume then increased until it reached a point that the bidding began in earnest. Negotiations flew like wind-blown sheet music, until the storm subsided.

Bob paid $75 for that non-descript frog: If it had been an original, with the key word being "if," it would have been worth many times that amount. Bob, however, was a law-enforcement officer who barely earned that much money in a week. I thought: 'All that cash for a wooden frog, and one with a questionable pedigree?' Incredulous, I bit my lip.

I had attempted to intervene from the start. However, Bob's a lot bigger than I am, and I was helpless in the wake of his collecting credentials. I planned to stop by my shop later on, where I intended to break the news.

That "news" was that I had a collection of 15 or 20 tackle boxes that customers had given me over the years. Several contained frogs of various descriptions, including the one that Bob had bought. The whole kit and caboodle, which I would have gladly given him, is now worth in the neighborhood of $20,000. Did you hear me say that I'd give it away? When Nicholson roared, you could hear him in Georgia.

However, even his ire couldn't quell the fervor that I'd seen in his eyes at the show. There's something special about collecting that's like an addiction, or respect for these artfully-crafted relics. It's not just a means to an end. A week or two later, I put my old tackle in order. The next thing I did was purchase a lifetime membership in the Florida Antique Tackle Collector's Association. By then, I was on my way.

❖   ❖   ❖

So why not join me in my inner office, where I keep most of the stuff I buy? I'm surrounded, you'll notice, by all sorts of tackle, including lures in boxes and yellowed magazines. Some of these items are classics, and worth plenty to the right collector. Yet a big game reel that's locked in a cabinet is the most-remarkable piece of all. Here's how it got where it is today:

Several years back, a widow approached me about purchasing some items from her late husband's estate. One immediately caught my eye: a huge silver trolling reel with metallic side plates that he had used to fish for bluefin tuna off the New Jersey coast. I'd read accounts of the Seabright fishery, and how men in dories rowed far out to sea. That, I recalled, was in the 1930's. The woman, I guessed, was in her nineties.

Now there on my desk sat this relic from the past, its spool filled to the brim with linen line. I couldn't help wondering about her late husband's exploits, and the catches he'd made with this heavy winch. Who could have ever envisioned the truth?

I invited the widow—an elegant lady—to join me for coffee while we sat there talking. It was then that the threads of this "tail" unraveled.

She confirmed my suspicion that her husband had caught tuna, but that his greatest catch was a dying man: one being swept out to sea. Were it not for him and this ancient winch, a life would have surely been lost. So here's her account, from the beginning, which I've never had reason to doubt:

At the time of the incident, she and her husband were living near an inlet on the Jersey Shore. When he wasn't out fishing, the two drove to the jetties to watch the dories working the rip.

On the day in question, ground swells were crashing, as small craft struggled against the tide. By then, the majority had turned around, but a few stalwart souls were inside the jetties.

Those were the days of striped bass and "tide-runners"—those magnificent weakfish that ran every fall. It was possible to catch a boatload back then, using nothing but a hand line and a block tin squid. Keep in mind that the times were hard, and practically everyone ate fish of some kind

Meanwhile, a fisherman was working the inlet, when one of his oars snapped in two and laid him cross-wise. Then a ground swell broke and filled the boat, before the one that followed rolled it over. Within seconds he was treading water, with nothing to do but hang on and pray. As the tide kept pushing the dory out to sea, it carried him farther from shore. The victim, it turned out, was a friend of her husband.

The lady and her husband, who looked on in horror, lived less than a mile away. So they high-tailed it home in search of a life preserver in the form of a rubber doughnut. That was back in the days of the original beach buggies, when everyone kept spare tubes for their tires—huge ones that were deliberately under-inflated—perfect for the task at hand.

"Go fetch my tuna rod," the man said to his wife, while he searched the basement for the giant tube. Then, with gear in tow, they raced back to the inlet, where the first thing he did was secure the line to the tube. Oblivious to the swells, he climbed onto the jetty and, with the help of several bystanders, tossed the tube to the current. Then he backed-off the drag and headed for shore, while scanning the beach for a dune.

By then, the victim had drifted a ways out to sea, as well as down the beach. Not only was he unable to make any headway, he was rapidly losing ground. The situation was now one of life and death, with the victim immersed in the icy water. Yet both husband and wife refused to relent.

Next, the man spied a dune and asked his wife to climb it, to where she'd be able to direct a rescue attempt. From there she could line-up the dory—with the floating tube and her husband's position. By moving up and down the surf, he could position the tube according to his wife's instructions. Free-spooling and slogging, reeling and pumping, while keeping the seaweed from ruining the drift—until the half-drowned victim could relinquish his hold and grab the redeeming doughnut. It took an hour from start to finish.

By now, you can guess the outcome, and how our hero cranked his "catch" to safety. That reel, incidentally, holds over 1,000 yards of line, most of which was used in the rescue. The man he saved, she told me later, lived for another 40 years.

She didn't want much for that reel. And now that I have it, I'm not inclined to sell it. Some things, like I said, transcend mere profit.

❖ ❖ ❖

You meet people while collecting who are true "class acts," in the most-demanding sense of the term

A perfect example lived on Hillsboro Mile: a lady who had

read my name in a newspaper article—one written by outdoors writer, Steve Waters of the *South Florida Sun-Sentinel*. The article had appeared five years earlier, but her husband had clipped and saved it. Now he was dead, and she was calling.

The article—which was all about collecting old tackle—listed my address and phone number, which hadn't changed in the interim. So I picked up the phone and introduced myself, while waiting to hear what she had to say: Was I interested in looking at some tackle?

I was indeed, and I'd drive to her home—a home she planned to vacate soon, when her condo on Hillsboro Inlet was finally finished. From her brief description, he'd left worthwhile gear. But all that glitters isn't gold.

Therein lies the rub: For all the antiques I buy and sell, I end-up disposing of a mountain of junk. Then, there's plenty of stuff that's not really collectible, which I give away to kids or charities. But like I said, you never know:

When I arrived at her home, I was duly impressed. Surrounded by the elegance of a bygone era, was a dignified woman if ever I've met one. Among the items she'd kept in a closet were several split-cane fly rods and valuable fly reels, along with some E.L. Baker surf rods and assorted salt water spinning gear. I offered her $5,000 for the lot, an offer she politely refused

"My husband said he wanted you to have it. You may not remember him, but he shopped in your store. All I ask is that you select a few items that my grandchildren can use when they come to visit. Pick-out something they can use in the surf, if you will. That's the kind of fishing my husband preferred."

I didn't know what to say.

"But, Ma'am, what you have here is all good stuff, and I'm more than willing to pay you for it."

"Nonsense" she countered, "I have all the money I need." She refused to listen to another word. So I sifted through the spoils of a sporting lifetime, and came-up with a few rods and reels, and a hip-roofed box that she could save for her grand kids.

I filled the trays with Pfleuger "Last Word" spoons, some Barracuda brand jigs, and assorted sinkers and hooks. When it came time to lug the rest to my car, I saw that her maid and gardener had already done it.

We said good-bye on the manicured lawn of the house where she'd spent the only life she knew. I watched her fight back the tears, as decades' worth of memories were set to roll down the driveway. She said she'd had everything a woman could want, but now her husband was gone. I hoped that someday the hurt would heal. Then, after she'd walked back inside, I found the maid and gardener, and handed each a handful of cash.

The last I heard, she'd moved into that condo, a million-dollar apartment overlooking the inlet. Now her grandsons could still visit whenever they wanted, and enjoy the same beachfront access as they had before. I pictured them casting and watching the girls, while she sat upstairs and painted or read—I can't remember which. But things don't always turn out that way.

I received another call from the same article. A widow in Parkland, a ways west of town, was faced with a similar situation. She wondered if I'd drive out and make her an offer on her deceased husband's gear. The address she gave me was halfway to Naples, so I decided to ask a few questions first.

"Oh yes," she assured me. "He had several bamboo rods just like you described—some with joints. And yes, the reels are in tip-top condition; in fact, they're still on the rods."

She'd said enough to trip my trigger, so I hopped in my car and headed west. An hour and a half later, I pulled up in front of what appeared to be a prestigious address. At this point my hopes were high.

She met me at the door before stepping outside, and taking me to an outside storage bin where the rods lay baking. But before you tear out your hair, you ought to know this:

Bamboo, yes; split-cane, no. Now picture those shafts, all varnished and shiny, that subsistence fishermen use in canals. It's a pastoral image that her husband enjoyed. In fact, the bobbers and hooks were still in place, where he must have left them on his final outing.

As far as the reels, they were actually bobbins, around which he'd wrapped his line. Neither gears nor clickers, nor any amenities, interrupted the simplicity of this primitive arrangement. The aggregate value of the entire "collection" was less than I'd spent on the gas to get there. Yet that, we acknowledge, is the price we pay when we choose to collect antique tackle.

There's a Latin phrase, "Caveat emptor," which loosely translated, means "Let the buyer beware." It's one we collectors need to keep in mind.

5

Bass, Boca, and My Beginnings

"While gators and garfish wallowed beneath us,
I got a whiff of swamp scent. To a lad my age,
it was pure adventure."

Photo by Pat Ford.

It all starts somewhere

Every story has a beginning: take the events that started me fishing. My earliest recollections are of a family in Boca who figure prominently in our little town's history. My mentor's father was J. W. Ash, the original bridge tender on the antiquated swing bridge that once spanned Boca Inlet. While I "earned my bones" fishing the salt, I cut my teeth in the marsh.

Boca Raton was an anachronism in those days—frozen in time in a part of Florida that was developing faster than a runaway bed sore. There weren't any boutiques or night clubs to speak of. In fact, only 2,000 residents lived in town when my family moved here in the late 1950's.

Maybe that's why we got to know one another, which is how my parents met Mr. Ash? It was his son, however, who asked me along to a place he referred to as Loxahatchee—a marsh located west of town. His entire family would be coming along. It was my very first outing, and I remember it fondly.

The details remain clear in my mind. The trip started early,

around 2 a.m., when Ash pulled-up in his old red truck. Since my
street was dark, it heightened the mystery, and while I didn't know
squat about bass at the time, I hoped that was about to change.

We took off down the tarmac, carrying a johnboat that he'd
lashed to the truck bed. A nine-horse outboard that he'd stuffed
beneath it rattled whenever we hit a bump. One of Ash's sons
rode back there for several hours in order to keep it from jostling
out. We eventually reached a road that pointed us westward and
pointed us towards the Everglades.

Eventually, it led to a levee—one of those earthen dikes that
holds back the swamp whenever the marsh fills to overflowing,
which is usually during the summer. A road of sorts ran along the
crest, although it hardly deserves such lofty distinction. "String
of potholes" would be a lot more-accurate. Yet ride it we did,
for what seemed like forever, until we reached the point where
it ended. It had run into another levee—one that stretched both
north and south—beyond which there was only water and weeds.
The swamp, quite literally, formed the horizon.

I couldn't believe my eyes: a sunken prairie all adrift with
green; plus, some taller plants that appeared to be rooted. The
latter looked a bit like giant grasses, but I had no idea what they
were at the time. No previous experience could have ever prepared me for this vista of watery expanse.

It was silent except for the birds, which were filling the air with
their interminable squawking. If the sun, in the meantime, was
barely up, who could ignore all the beating wings? While gators
and garfish wallowed beneath us, I got my first whiff of swamp

scent. To a lad my age, it was pure adventure. More than ever now, I wanted to fish.

I helped Ash and his sons slide the boat off the truck, before he clamped the outboard to the wooden transom. Then we loaded our gear, which included a cooler and stove, before dragging the boat to the edge of the marsh. Mrs. Ash would help, too, but that would come later. After Ash shoved the bow through some water hyacinths, he climbed aboard near the stern.

Then he yanked the pull-cord and we all got in, and moments later, we were chugging along, and crossing what looked like open water. He then ran us aground on a hammock, where the sloping bottom would make wading easier. After we all jumped out and the boys started casting, Mrs. Ash lit the Coleman stove.

Her husband had rigged us with Johnson "Silver Minnows"—similar to the ones in use today—which he tipped with Uncle Josh pork chunks. I would later learn more of the whys and wherefores, but now all I wanted was to catch a fish—any fish, it didn't matter. The reels we were using were standard fare—Pflueger Supreme bait casters, if my memory serves me—and our rods had pistol grip handles. The lines, I recall, were black braided nylon.

Ashe caught a bass within the first few minutes: a healthy specimen of three or four pounds. Then he followed it up with a second. It wasn't long afterwards that one hit my spoon, in spite of my questionable casting. My hands started shaking when I tried to reel; in fact, I let go of the handle a time or two. After rapping my knuckles, I managed to beach what turned out to be a nice-sized bass.

The determined jumps, the dogged resistance; clearly the most fun I'd ever had. Then and there, I was hooked.

We allowed those bass to flop on the bank, before Ashe took them back to the boat—where he showed me how to fillet a fish. I remember his homemade foredeck, where he skinned the fillets, before tossing the carcasses into the water. He was deliberate but careful, and wasted no time in getting those fillets on ice. I was impressed by the impromptu surgery lesson.

Yet something that haunts me after all those years is the image of those carcasses lying on the bottom. Call it a figment of my imagination, but they appeared to still be alive—breathing like zombies in some Hollywood horror film. It was no doubt the result of the shifting boat, which created a miniature current. It's funny, when you're a kid, what sticks in your mind.

We went back to fishing, while Mrs. Ashe cooked.

She'd brought cornmeal along in a plastic bag, and enough eggs, bacon and potatoes to feed a regiment—and, of course, vegetable oil and a skillet. Just thinking about it still makes my mouth water. We ate in that al fresco setting, while mallards and teal flew by overhead. No feast I've enjoyed will ever compare. Our watches had yet to read 8:00 a.m.

Recalling that day still raises some questions, like what turned a single trip into a lifetime obsession? Was it the thrill of conquering those creatures of the wild, or just the camaraderie and all that food? Or the total spell of the Great Outdoors? It's definitely worth additional research, but whatever the verdict, it worked for me.

Not long afterwards, I was fishing regularly and within a month, I had a job—at Boca Tackle on Palmetto Park Road. We lived near the center of town, but I fished for bass wherever I could, providing I could find productive water. One place that qualified wasn't all that far, which leads to the following "tail."

❖ ❖ ❖

In the early 1960's, a Mrs. Baker shopped in our store. She lived with her husband on Boca Lake—a prestigious address, if you don't know the area. The Bakers had amassed a fortune, allowing Helen to indulge her hobby, which, if you haven't guessed, was fishing.

You could say I was the grandson she never had, but it worked to our mutual advantage. She was fishing at the time with the Palm Beach crowd, which typically meant trolling for sailfish. But as I got to know her, I was pleased to discover that her interests strayed beyond spindle-beaks. Here are a few examples:

We'd fish for snook off her dock in the Lake, and I spoke with her husband about tarpon and trout. Plus, she confessed that she'd drive her brand new car—a shiny white Thunderbird that her husband had bought her—all the way to Lake Okeechobee in order to fish for bass. She'd hire a guide, and from what she said, land bass of up to four or five pounds. That was all the incentive I needed.

I invited her to join me at the Boca "Muck Pit," a name synonymous with lunker bass. As you're about to read, I had reason to believe that at least one real monster lurked in its depths.

So what made the Muck Pit so special? For starters, it was the largest lake in Boca, and located conveniently near the center of town—not far from where 28th Street crosses Dixie Highway. The pit got its name from construction interests that mined its depths for muck and fill. That was 30 years earlier. Now cattails surrounded its periphery, and the only access was via a muddy trail that entered from Dixie Highway.

As far as the Mud Pit's claim to fame: Someone had stocked it with largemouth bass that kept on growing in the fertile environment. That piqued Helen's interest.

She'd pick me up after school in her car, and we'd splash through the mud all the way to the water. Then we'd wade the shallows, while the sun was setting, and more often than not release a mess of bass. If you hadn't fished the pit in those days, you wouldn't believe the numbers. Not in a city that's known for its chic.

As in most manmade pits, there's a drop-off, beyond which bass retreat when the sun's overhead. But just after dawn, then again at dusk, they enter the shallows to feed—usually just outside the cattails. So that's where we'd cast our lures. Those were the days when a woman like Helen could fish places like this without any problem. We did, however, cross a single hurdle.

I remember a curious cottonmouth that we encountered in ankle-deep water. The snake, which apparently was looking for dinner, came dangerously close to ruining our day. Or worse, I shudder to think. I was wearing a pair of shorts at the time.

Forget what you've heard about snakes underwater, or that

they won't strike without provocation. Their definition may differ from ours. How, for example, can they feed on fish without ever having to open their mouths? I was wading barefoot and watching my line, when I felt something heavy against my foot. When I paused to look, I discovered this monster that had apparently decided to park there. It began furtively tonguing my calf. All I could do was close my eyes.

My hands started shaking and I nearly passed-out, as the snake's tongue kept working higher, until eventually reaching my knee. Perhaps it was tasting my perspiration, which was about to be joined by something less-pleasant? Then it lowered back down on my right foot, before retracing its route up my opposite leg. That snake, let me tell you, was huge.

Its body was so wide that it obscured my toes, which now lay pinioned in the urine-stained water. Yet what could I do but stand perfectly still? What were probably minutes felt like hours, while all I braced for the worst. I was 13 years old at the time.

The snake remained parked on both of my feet, while I desperately sought a solution. Eventually, however, I followed my instincts, by waiting until its weight was nearly centered, then jumping as high as I could—while kicking-out violently with both of my legs. It took every ounce of my strength, and I fell back on my butt.

For a moment, I lay there dazed and sputtering, until Mrs. Baker could help me up. I'm not sure which one of us was shaking the most. That kick launched the snake into deeper water, and paved the way for our hasty retreat.

While escaping unscathed was the bottom line, Mrs. Baker admitted that her greatest fear was explaining my death to my mother. Who, after all, had driven me there? That broke the tension, and we both started laughing. Did I mention that she paid me to guide her?

I made $1.10/ hour in the shop at the time, a rate that Mrs. Baker was happy to quadruple. But more than the money, our friendship allowed me to fish without having to walk or ride my bike all the time. And for her to catch bass much closer to home. I think they call the process symbiosis. As a bonus, her husband ordered an all-white rod, one of the first I built at our shop. You can guess what he wanted to match.

Mrs. Baker and I enjoyed some wonderful fishing, all the more remarkable in our own backyard. Incidentally, she usually opted for spinning gear—and reels like the Mitchell, Quick, or Alcedo—to cast the light lures she used on Okeechobee.

She carried me up there several times, an experience I enjoyed immensely. As for me? I'm a fan of casting tackle and surface plugs—having caught two bass at a time on several occasions, once at the Muck Pit.

Mrs. Baker landed some "nice" bass in her time, but never the trophy she so desperately wanted, like the fish I'd seen on a previous outing. Now try to picture the following:

❖   ❖   ❖

Since no one in my family was landed gentry, my mother—a devout Southern Baptist from South Carolina—cooked redwing blackbirds from an early age. I hunted them in the local marshes, including the one that surrounded the Muck Pit. It was just a further attempt to bring home the bacon. But what bird hunters learn—whether we like it or not—is that we don't always kill our targets. Which leads to the following "tail:"

I'd just knocked one down, in the days before Helen, when the largest bass I could ever imagine appeared on top and swallowed it whole. And all I could do was stand there gaping. But several years later, while I was hunting that spot, I got what I think was a second chance. However,I was with my brother, and we retrieved that bird.

By then, he'd heard about the monster bass, and how it had swallowed the redwing. While we had no fishing gear per se in the truck, my brother, who was working in the trades at the time, always kept a chalk line. Along with a box that contained a few fish hooks.

We viewed that bird as an omen. So while taking care not to harm it, we attached one leg with a rubber band to a hook that we'd tied to the chalk line. We then pulled off some line and freed it, and it immediately swam for the nearest cattail.

Halfway there, it, too, disappeared, as a monster bass gave an encore performance. But fortunately for the redwing, the bass coughed it up the instant we tightened the chalk line.

That bass, which we agreed had eaten his last redwing, tipped the scales at nearly 13 pounds. Could it have been a coincidence, or do other monsters lurk in the depths of that muddy pit? You decide for yourself. Bass, it turns out, are the stuff of legends, and also a part of our local history.

"Pound for pound, and inch for inch, the gamest fish that swims." That's how Dr. Edward Henshall described America's black bass in his "Book of the Black Bass" (published in 1881). At the time he was writing about the smallmouth bass, a cold-water species you won't find here in Florida. However, our lowly largemouths—if that's how you see them—have been drawing the crowds for years—Dr. Henshall included. I mention this because so few of our citizens recognize the largemouth's role in our local history.

Names like the Muck Pit and Loxahatchee seem far removed to the throngs of tourists. Yet to kids like me who embraced the outdoors, they keep the legend alive—a legend of wild and unfettered spaces where wildlife abounds: something most folks won't find close to home.

6

MOUTH OF THE RAT?

"The original Boca Inlet bridge."

How shifting inlet helped shape a town

When Florida was part of the Spanish Empire, the Conquistadors referred to "Boca Ratones." Were they talking about tiny Boca Inlet—or rock formations located farther south that nibbled at the hulls of their ships? The term literally translated means "mice mouth." But either interpretation evokes our history.

The easternmost edge of the Florida peninsula is bordered by barrier islands separated from the mainland by shallow lagoons, including the Indian and Banana Rivers and farther south, the Spanish. Unlike in the Gulf, with its low-energy shorelines, Atlantic beaches are characterized by dunes that are formed by the action of the wind and the waves. It's through these build-ups that the lagoons and sea meet via a series of natural inlets. It's been that way for millions of years.

Such an inlet figures prominently in Boca Raton's history. While originally a trickle that drained ancient Lake Boca, it kept shifting and re-forming until someone dredged it—and opened the mainland to wealthy tourists who flocked to the region in their luxury yachts. That was back in the 1920's, in the midst of the Florida land boom. To picture the transition is to look back in time to when Boca as we know it was still part wilderness.

What was later to become a "town of distinction" consisted of a few scattered farms. Excavations confirm that Native Americans walked these warrens prior to Columbus' voyage. But the first white settlers didn't arrive until later—the 1880's to be exact—only slightly ahead of the railroad. So it was pineapples and not pomp that drew the crowds, if you forgive the alliteration. The Florida East Coast Railroad, which was Henry Flagler's "baby," wasn't completed until several years later. But getting back to the inlet. . . .

You didn't just go to the beach back then, or drive to the inlet, either. What's now a five-minute car ride required a morning's effort that included crossing Lake Boca by rowboat before traversing the dunes on foot. Folks had to struggle to reach the ocean, but by all accounts, they came in droves to enjoy the sand and the surf. That part hasn't changed in the interim. Plus, an added incentive was the wonderful fishing, which for shore-based anglers, meant windrows of bluefish. That's how it was when my family moved here back in the 1950's.

My first real job was at Boca Tackle, located on historic Palmetto Park Road. Fortuitously, Palmetto led straight to the beach and therefore, the inlet bridge on A-1-A. That old wooden swing bridge was a bona fide classic, left over from the 1920's.

Its creosoted pilings and a hand-driven mechanism were relics of a bygone era. It was the son of the original bridge tender, a local fixture named Hayden Ashe, who started me fishing in earnest.

It was my first experience with a rod and reel, and a classic example of "love at first bite." Plus, it whetted my appetite for fishing the salt.

I was 11 years old when I started that job, and it wasn't long afterwards that I bought a bike. When I finished my shift, I'd peddle to the beach, and past the pavilion to a rock formation that we all referred to as Butt's Cave. That's where the incoming breakers were funneled through the rocks, and the spaces between them literally teemed with mullet—during the fall migration.

The Butts family, who came here as farmers, once owned that stretch of beach. Whether our early residents regaled in their pedigrees isn't a matter of debate. However, just like in Boston or New York City, they made our town what it is today—the jewel envisioned by Addison Mizner, the architect who designed the Cloisters Hotel.

The Cloisters, which sits across from the inlet, was later renamed the Boca Hotel and Club. It's still there today. In fact, my family moved here from North Carolina, just so my father could work there. The Inlet itself and the surrounding beaches host another migration that's just as predictable—albeit from a different perspective.

If you're looking for superlatives, simply say "Mullet Run"— especially to anyone who's fished it: I've watched mullet schools from September to Thanksgiving that stretched from the surf to a quarter mile offshore, and as far north and south as I was able to see. Those living carpets attract throngs of predators that gorge on the baitfish that keep moving south.

What bears a surprising resemblance to breaking snowballs sends the mullet flying, as predators attack from below. Snook, jacks and sharks made a real commotion, while tarpon flashed in the afternoon sunlight. Every few seconds, one takes to the air. And yes, there were plenty of bluefish—more than anyone wanted to catch. Blues typically hit anything that moves. They, like the others, entered the inlet.

Butt's Cave was the perfect vantage point, especially during the mullet run. The finger mullet got so thick in the crannies that I could scoop them up with my dip net. But when I tossed one out from that rocky platform, I had no idea what to expect: The first cast, a bluefish; the second, a snook, as giant tarpon flashed through the schools. I'd hook them, also, on numerous occasions, and once or twice I managed to land one.

It's strange, when you think how removed it all seems: a time when our lives were centered in town. Then beachfront property became all the rage; and freedom of access, a thing of the past. But for a very brief time we had it all.

Just remembering my boss at Boca Tackle brings back a flood of memories. His name was Bill Kane, and we sold live shrimp—although the shop had no salt water well. That meant changing the water by hand, a feat we accomplished by drawing it elsewhere and trucking it back to our concrete shrimp tank.

We pumped water from Boca Inlet, at least twice a week, by

filling a well in the back of Bill's truck that closely resembled a coffin. We'd fill-up on the incoming tide to take advantage of the cleaner water. My job was to position the hose, while Bill was in charge of the pump. He'd park the truck alongside the bridge.

I'd hide a rod and reel in the back, and sneak-in some casts while the pump was running. Since filling the well took nearly an hour, I had plenty of time to prospect. I discovered many a marvel there in the current: schools of leopard rays and giant barracudas; then, later on—when I learned what to look for—thousands of snook. Like they say, the wonders never ceased.

The incoming tide propelled them towards my post. You could compare it to a three-dimensional sideshow, or streaming video in the days before our modern technology. Then the water turned brown when the tide reversed.

Over years of fishing that inlet, I caught plenty of snook and other large game fish—usually on the outgoing tide. Two jacks I remember tipped the scales at over 50 pounds apiece. However, few thrills compared to those first tiny "bait-stealers" that I tricked as a kid with bits of dead shrimp. That's before I discovered salt water lures.

When I made that leap my tackle expanded, but not as fast as my aspirations. Between snook on the jetty and jacks in the "lake," I always had something to fish for. The old wooden swing bridge was eventually replaced by a bascule structure. But we learned how to fish that one, too. It all came down to a basic premise:

Inlets are special places. They connect the sea with our inland waters, but sometimes they close, leaving inshore waters literally landlocked. So any fish that pass between the lagoon and the sea have their access denied. Once-thriving conduits become festering swill. In fact, your sense of smell may be the first indication that this natural exchange has been put on hold.

Around the time I was attending junior college, Boca Inlet decided to close. That was back in the 1960's. For several years prior, it had been losing depth, due to a build-up of sand.

When it closed-off completely, Boca Lake became stagnant—untenable, especially with no relief in sight. If you're at all familiar with our local geography, you know that the two closest inlets—Hillsboro and Boynton—lie 20 miles apart in opposite directions. So the Intracoastal Waterway lost most of its current, the kiss of death for snook at the inlet.

Other things died—including our business—since when no one caught fish, they didn't buy bait, or the various sundries that fishermen carry. So what kind of crowd did we cater to previously? I'll give you a few examples:

One hundred or more cars lined Boca Lake during the famous pompano runs. Then, plenty of folks fished the inlet on weekends. Take kids like me who dabbled with shrimp, or the families who came to enjoy the beach. However you looked at it, we needed that inlet.

Enter Tony Plungus, from Boca Tackle. He was younger than me, but an avid fisherman, and his father was a professor at

Florida Atlantic University. I recall another guy, too—a customer who worked for IBM. I'd been teaching him how to fish for snook (my specialty, if you hadn't guessed) before the inlet closed. The gist of the story is that we all got together and decided it needed re-opening—regardless of what it took.

It was early summer, and the groundswells had subsided. So according to plan, we met just after daybreak before marching to the source of the problem. A sandbar now blocked the entrance of the inlet all the way from the mouth to the turn—a distance of 200 yards.

The sand was piled as high as the dunes. Yet the best we could muster were hoes and shovels. Our plan was to dig a trench from the mouth to where the sandbar tapered-off into Boca Lake. We hoped that the tide, which had recently turned, would help us accomplish our task. I'll never forget those first few minutes.

We stood sweating with the sun to our backs, long yards to go with no time-outs. Were we fools to challenge the power of Nature? Read on, then decide for yourself. Meanwhile, we chose to start digging despite the odds, so we picked a starting point between the jetties, and 50 feet from where the waves were breaking.

At 10:00 a.m. we were joined by others—at least 30 volunteers who responded to the call that we'd posted all over town. Many of these folks had been affected by the closure, but we hadn't expected a response like this. By noon that number had increased even further—to an incredible crowd of 500 people, who came armed with pitchforks, hoes, and shovels. And anything else they could carry.

We were determined to open that inlet, which at that point had been closed for nearly a year. With all the digging, sand started flying and for once, our spirits soared.

Imagine an ant hill filled with people: That's how we must have looked. While some volunteers dragged the sand away, others continued to dig it. The second group used buckets and shovels, while the first—who were forced to improvise—relied on pails, palm fronds, and blankets—anything they could cover with sand. While some piles imploded, most of them didn't.

By 6:00 p.m., we had completed a trench that was 50 feet wide and several feet deep. It ran all the way from the surf to the bend, at a time when the tide started rising.

In a last-ditch effort (so-to-speak), we rushed to the mouth and started digging towards the breakers like men possessed. And all the while, the sea kept rising—cooling our legs with its promise.

The breakers kept pushing farther inland, and by dark the first green water in over a year had forced its way into Boca Lake. The higher it rose, the faster it came. Our makeshift channel kept getting deeper and deeper and by dawn, the current flowed in both directions.

A day or two later, the city responded by sending a bulldozer to pile-up the sand. But volunteers had accomplished much of the task with determination and little else. What they'd faced, however, was the result of a dynamic that repeats itself over time.

During winter, the swells chew off tons of sand that gets carried away by the current. Then spring returns, with its southerly breezes, and the sand settles back into place. What we refer to as our "long-shore current" typically runs from south to north. That's why jetties and beaches on the north side of inlets extend farther from shore than their southerly counterparts. While sandbars cause their share of aggravation, ours was the stuff of a legend or two.

A local character that was larger than life left his mark on our inlet. I refer to Jim Smith, angler-extraordinaire and owner of the Jim Smith Boat Works, and the Bluefin Motel, on Boca Beach. Jim, we had heard, raced boats in the past. By the time I met him, he and *Boca Jima*—his 39-foot sport fisherman powered by twin "Triple Nickel" Detroit diesels—had become local fixtures if we ever had one.

Jim sported an artificial leg—a prosthetic testimony to life in the fast lane. According to one report, he lost it in a boating accident, while another hinted at motorcycles. Either way, he liked to go fast.

He'd come into our shop nearly every day and regale us with tales of his offshore exploits. To a teenager like me, Jim was a god. When he wasn't chasing tuna or marlin in the Bahamas, he'd run the local beaches in search of cobia.

Cobia or "ling," are outstanding table fare, something that few people realized at the time. They're also renowned for their fighting ability, and their habit of following sting rays. Rays show-up against sandy bottoms, especially from elevated vantage points—something that Jim had covered in spades.

He'd work his magic from a tuna tower that had no equal

when it came to height. Jim had personally designed *Boca Jima,* and tuna towers—built for pursuing their namesake—were glorified aluminum scaffolds. The idea behind them is to provide increased visibility for whoever is running the boat.

Jim's tower had a chain-driven elevator lift that helped him to reach his lofty perch. He'd frequently take guests from the motel, and run the shallows north to Palm Beach. That's where he'd spot all the sting rays.

He was as good as it gets at finding cobia, and he brought back the evidence to prove it. So when he asked me to join him one day in the shop, I could barely contain my excitement. We'd give the ling a licking; I could hardly sleep that night.

Let me preface what follows by explaining that the inlet was closing, but not completely like it had before. Still, less than two feet of water covered the sandbar at the top of the incoming tide. The bridge hadn't opened in months, and most folks figured it was because of the sandbar. High tide the next morning was at 7:30 A.M.

We left Jim's dock on Boca Lake just after daybreak. I guessed we'd head out Hillsboro Inlet, before working our way north to Boynton, then returning home in the Intracoastal. So when Jim requested that I take the wheel, and pointed me straight for Boca Inlet Bridge, I didn't know what to expect.

What could he have in mind? While we sat there idling in Boca Lake, Jim blew the horn for the bridge to open. After five minutes passed with no response, he ordered me up in the tower—armed with an old-fashioned air horn, along with instructions on what to do. It was scary at first, but exciting, too. Then, Jim took the controls and drove me so close to the fender that I could practically touch the bridge tender's office.

From my elevated position I could see that worthy—sound asleep in his chair. The bridge, after all, hadn't opened in months, due to the absence of nautical traffic. So according to plan, I held out the horn and positioned it near the window. All it took was a single blast to launch the bridge tender like a Polaris missile.

He must have figured that a truck jumped the curb, and flattened the office with him inside it. And that the sound he'd heard was Gabriel's Trump, welcoming him into Glory.

When he looked out the window, Jim was standing beneath him with a strident request to open that bridge. I'll spare you the actual verbage. The bridge tender, who knew not to argue, got to the business at hand.

I watched with amusement as he lowered both turnstiles, while traffic on A-1-A ground to a halt. One car in particular, a white Continental, was sitting second in line when a man jumped out, and started shouting and waving in an attempt to warn us. We heard him yell that there wasn't enough water to allow us to clear the inlet.

"We're just looking," was all Jim said in response.

We cleared the bridge and motored forward in all that remained of a narrow channel. I recall it running along the south jetty, just where it is today. Meanwhile, Jim took my place in the tower, after ordering me down to the bridge. I'm thankful he did, as you'll see for yourself.

It was November or December—I can't remember which—

and groundswells were rolling ashore in green lines. They broke harmlessly over the sandbar, their energy squandered in smears of foam. At this point, we were barely moving—marking the bottom by bumping our keel.

I could feel each time we hit the sandbar, but Jim didn't seem concerned. We nudged it again a few more times, before eventually running aground. Jim remained stoic throughout these maneuvers. Then, after looking around, he eased both engines into reverse, and backed us up to the bend in the inlet, a distance of 200 yards. Our retreat, in the meantime, created a wake that rebounded off the jetties.

Jim took the engines out of gear again, and allowed the stern to settle. We idled momentarily while he timed the swells, before he hollered to us all to: "Hold on tight." He then gunned both engines in forward, but as we approached the sandbar, he pulled back hard.

That allowed our wake to push us across. Then, just as the props cleared the worst of the sandbar, he pushed both throttles down really hard. I can still recall the way everything shuddered, as the hull rose-up and started to sprint. Who could forget the whine of those "Triple Nickels," or the rooster tail that shot from our stern? Smith had effectively cleared the inlet; leaving a contrail of diesel fumes.

Boca Jima jumped like a jackrabbit, as her bow dug into the oncoming swells. And before I knew it, we were skimming along in water so shallow that a kid could cross it—without ever getting his shirt wet.

I gripped the rail with my white-knuckled hands, and shut my eyes in abject terror. While I have no idea how fast we were running, it had to be more than 30 knots. I've since discovered a video of *Boca Jima* blasting across Boca Lake. It still gives me chills to watch it.

After clearing the inlet at break-neck speed, Jim turned the wheel to the north. Then, in less than a minute, we were cruising along as if this defining moment had never happened. I doubt if he ever flinched—or made further comment about this miraculous escape, which no lesser captain would have ever attempted. Jim designed *Boca Jima* from tower to keel, and he was fully-aware of its capabilities. However, speaking for myself, it took awhile before the blood returned to my legs.

No boat of any size had been through Boca Inlet for several months prior to our miraculous escape. As additional testimony to Jim's ability, he immediately found a school of cobia, just north of the inlet we'd so recently breeched. Our take for that day was over 40 fish, all of which weighed between 30 and 50 pounds.

We worked or way north to Boynton Inlet, before ducking inside and running back home. Of the seven or eight of us on board at the time, no one touched Jim's dock with greater sense of relief. Or a higher regard for the legendary captain who made his home on Boca Lake.

Boca Inlet remains open for business, as do I in Lighthouse Point. With that in mind, I dedicate these "tails" of the inlet to the citizens of Boca—some of whom still refer to the "Mouth of the Rat."

Unwelcome Mat: This giant stingray hit a live bait intended for a snook. It took Tom Greene, Jim Roller and Jim Wise—who had no idea what they'd hooked—an entire night to subdue the monster. The battle shifted back and forth between Juno Pier and the surf.

Snook stalker threesome: From left: Tom, Don Caylor, Bill Nahrstedt. All fish caught on plug tackle.

Every so often, Boca Inlet becomes blocked by sand that's carried by the long-shore current. In one of Tom's chapters, the inlet is re-opened by individuals armed with shovels, buckets, and makeshift tools.

In the 60's, blocked Boca Inlet aerial view.
Same problem; different view.

Another view of a plugged Boca Inlet.

Photos on this page courtesy of the Boca Raton Historical Society.

Tom, with a 39 1/2 pound snook from Boynton Inlet.

Photo courtesy of Tom Greene

The ancient wooden, single lane bridge that spanned Boca Inlet was built after World War I. It was replaced by a concrete structure in the early 1960's.

Photo by T.P. Wyatt, courtesy of Tom Greene

Tom and Scott Hitch with limits of snook. The fish were from bridges in Stuart, Florida.

Tom's brother, Martin, with a snook and his dog, Chief.

Snook on a stick—plus, a 39 pound jack - with Kent Griffiths (L) and Tom.

Jack Hutton photo, courtesy of Tom Greene.

This Daytona 500 car was owned and driven by Tom's longtime friend, and fisherman, Jim Ingalls. Note the name on the side.

Photo courtesy of Tom Greene

Fred Walsh during the Mullet Run Tarpon.

Tom Green's brother, Russell, with a pair of snook.

Tom's nephews, Jonathan and Aaron Kline, with a bass.

A nice haul of bass. Left to right, Dale Flickenger, Joe Munson, and Tom Greene.
Dale helped Tom catch his first snook, see what he started?! Photo courtesy of Tom Greene

Russell Greene relaxes at Highland Beach, in Florida Bay, after releasing a 100 pound
tarpon on plug casting tackle, he had to lay down, he was so worn out.

Photo by Tom Greene

Captain Art and Captain Andy Bellisari of Boca, while filming the
TV show, *Fishing Fever.*

Nine snook weighing over 30 pounds apiece caught by Tom Greene and Murray Shatt.
It was possible to catch double limits by fishing before and then after midnight.

Bridge snook go ballistic as a mullet school passes.

Dave Brace photo, courtesy of Tom Greene

Young Steve Bellisari, later the quarterback for Ohio State, poses with his first sailfish.

Tom with a 39-1/2 pound snook, Port Everglades, Florida.

Photos courtesy of Tom Greene

Joe Munson, with a winning blue marlin he caught in the Bahamas, at the 1982 B.B.C. Tournament.

The bridges of the Overseas Highway, as it follows the sunset into the Gulf of Mexico.

Photo by Pat Ford

All in a night's work. Tom Greene and George Copeland catch from local bridges in South Florida.

Photo courtesy of Tom Greene

Jungle giant: Tom, with 25 pound peacock from Brazil's Rio Negro.

Tom's friend, Andy Bean, with an almost identical peacock from
the Rio Negro.

Photos courtesy of Tom Greene

Sam Snead delights the crowd.

Pro golfer, Andy Bean, slams one down the fairway.

Tom and son, Marlin, admires his first snook.

Joe Munson catches something other than blue marlin. He just loves to fish.

Tom and Michele Greene with bass from Lake Ida.

Photo by Tom Ryan

Now 30 years later, they still come around—only this time with kids of their own,
who love fishing as much as they do. Kids are always welcome.

Photo courtesy of Tom Greene

Tom clears his cast net, while he waits for a school of mullet to pass.

7

Spillway Chronicles

"Tom, with a snook at the Boynton Spillway"

Photo by Tom Ryan, courtesy of Tom Greene.

Where fresh meets salt, or something like it.

The Everglades, essentially, is a meandering river that empties into Florida Bay. However, when its headwaters overflow due to summer downpours, excess run-off takes a different route–towards Florida's heavily-populated southeast coast. A catastrophic flood during the 1920's claimed the lives of 1,500 farm workers. Now, thanks to a network that we take for granted, that run-off has been contained.

I refer specifically to South Florida Water Management District canals that connect to the salt through a series of spillways. These spillways do more than just re-direct rainwater. It's there, for example, that forage accumulates before sweeping downstream into the mouths of predators.

Threadfin and gizzard shad rank among the former, while tarpon and snook are major consumers. The structures themselves are concrete buttresses, equipped with gates that open on command. When Water Management personnel give the signal, the dinner bell rings for predators downstream, as well as for anglers who line the tailrace. So how do these openings affect "snook-heads" like me?

Well, the place where I live is laced with canal which were dug for water escapement. So I have plenty of access to spillways that attract snook, and I've enjoyed spectacular fishing at times when they opened, on live bait and lures–all types of tackle. It's not fishing that you'll find everyday, but it produces the size and the numbers that snook addicts crave.

❖   ❖   ❖

My earliest recollections of fishing a spillway date back to my teenage years. I'd already developed an addiction to snook, which drove me towards larger fish and greater numbers. Any kindred spirits know why snook are popular, but as far as the spillways, I had plenty to learn. Let me set the stage:

I'd fish Lake Worth Pier during summer vacation, back in the days when we "slew" the snook. Those pier snook, however, were unique in certain regards. Take their habit of schooling and their reluctance to hit. Not to mention that the schools stayed far enough from the pier to put a premium on Olympian casting. That pier, incidentally, sits just south of Palm Beach, and juts out to sea from the same barrier island. But back to those snook at the pier.

Every so often, the jacks or bonito (technically, false albacore) would drive schools of baitfish past where the snook were lying–at which time the snook fed on top. Make a heroic heave–with a live thread-fin herring or Spanish sardine rigged below a sliding sinker–and you'd immediately hook a 12 to 18-pounder. During "bait runs" the snook were easy to see, as they performed their signature somersaults. But most of the time, they lay there skulking.

Yet snook, like most fish, are opportunists that take advantage of the right conditions–the premise that lies at the heart of this story.

While I'm not trying to minimize the pier scenario, there's a downside that made a major difference: namely, that we seldom caught any trophies on the pier–which is where the Lake Worth Spillway came in. I'd been hearing about it from friends that I fished with, who regaled me with tales of their 35-pounders. While a mystique of sorts surrounded this structure, parts of it bear repeating. So first of all where is the spillway located?

Across Lake Worth Lagoon and several miles north, you'll see a lone canal that enters from the west. It's unremarkable except for one thing: It drains Palm Beach County's western environs. That's important during summer downpours, in order to keep the rain from flooding the streets. Need I remind you that near-daily deluges afflict South Floridians during the rainy season?

The spillway itself sits near the mouth of the canal, slightly upstream from the "Lake." So there isn't much current on the downstream side until the flood gates open. Then the tailrace becomes a raging torrent, with its surface awash in foam. The incredible force of the current is essentially a double-edged sword.

I mention that mostly as the preamble to a horrific event that I witnessed in person–although I wasn't quite sure what I was seeing at first. If my memory serves me, it was during my initial visit. The upshot of the story is that a young man drowned while trying to retrieve his lure. You wonder how such tragedies happen.

The spillway consisted of two separate sections: a larger one that housed the floodgates, and an auxiliary sluice that handled any overflow. The second of the two–which flowed over rip-rap– was shallow enough to wade: something the victim attempted to do and that cost him his life in the process. Most of what follows I learned later on.

Apparently, he'd been casting a heavy lure, which he managed to snag on the bottom. But when he waded out in an attempt to free it, he was unable to do so by jerking his rod. At a loss, he bent down with his face to the water, and began groping around in the bottom. It was then that his wrist became entangled in something–possibly discarded fishing line–and he subsequently lost his footing.

He was rapidly dragged under by the force of the current, and before anyone could get to him, he drowned.

I tell this both as a cautionary tale, and to emphasize the power of the moving water. I've witnessed similar accidents, I regret to say, and they're something you never forget. As I recall, everyone quit fishing that day.

❖ ❖ ❖

I eventually learned how to catch more and bigger snook, which is what brought me to spillways to begin with. First, I'd catch gizzard shad by throwing my cast net, then fish them live below the spillway. Don't confuse this filter-feeding forage species with its ocean-run cousin that anglers pursue. Meanwhile, snook hit shad whenever the gates are open, regardless of time or tide. And when you're fishing a bait that weighs nearly a pound, you don't have to worry about "throwbacks."

We catch "shad" by throwing our nets in the tailrace, and target ones that have passed through the spillway. The ideal bait measures between nine and 13 inches long. It's imperative to aim at breaks in the current–the one place the shad can hold. Then, as soon as we pluck one out of the net, we rush downstream and fish it.

If any of you are aspiring spillway fishermen, here's something you need to know: We hook gizzard shad through the nostrils, like "whitebait" on the pier.

Spillway snook follow the drop-offs, or hug the bottom in the lee of obstructions. These irregularities create "hydraulic cushions," where the current isn't so strong. If there's a trick to catching these opportunists, it's in tossing your shad directly upstream, where the churning maelstrom forces it downwards.

Snook that hold in these "kill zones" will spot the cripples and hurriedly gulp them down. Another technique is to walk the bank while allowing your shad to swim down off the ledge. When a big snook "thumps" it, we strike back hard with gear that could hoist a canoe.

Like an actual example? Then, take my friend Tom Mears, who's built like a line-backer in the NFL. He'd had plenty of experience fishing offshore, but he hadn't landed a trophy snook. But it did turn out that he owned a johnboat powered by a 9.8 HP outboard.

I made my mind up to assist Tom in his quest. We'd use the johnboat to fish the Boynton Spillway, where the snook, I'd heard, were stacked-up like cord wood. We launched at the ramp near the Lantana Bridge, before heading south to the spillway canal.

Canals below spillways are blocked by barrels that are tethered in a series to a heavy steel cable. It's a safety measure that I'm sure has saved lives. Back then, however, there were no such precautions, so we were able to approach to within yards of the gates. But after several hours of casting lures, the best we could do were three 8 to 10-pounders–not what I'd call a trophy.

I explained to Tom that our luck might change if I could manage to net some live bait. So I unfurled my 12-foot cast net and started throwing. I knew that some real monsters were lurking nearby, and that all we needed was a few live shad. But after a dozen throws in the raging current, all I could muster was a single pair. All that effort, in the meantime, had worn me out.

So I hooked-up a shad on my 10-foot bridge rod, and handed the outfit to Tom, who proceeded to toss it upstream–where a 30-pounder immediately gulped it. On that ungainly rod and 100-pound test, it was all Tom could do to stay in the boat. But after turning us around in circles, the snook eventually came to the transom–where, unfortunately, the hook pulled free. Then, a moment later, I missed a strike, at which time we were officially out of bait.

Try as I might, I couldn't net more shad, so I decided to hatch an elaborate plot. We'd head back to the ramp, put the boat on the trailer, then drive to the spillway canal; but this time we'd launch on the upstream side. I was convince if we did this that I could net more bait.

The plan came together like a Swiss watch. I headed for a place where two canals meet that the locals refer to as "Four Points." After tucking the drawstrings on my very first throw, I could barely recover my net–thanks to 40 shad that were flopping wildly. We quickly scooped them into our garbage can bait well before heading back to the ramp.

After loading the johnboat back on the trailer, we hurriedly drove to Lantana, where we launched again and re-traced our steps. But this time, with a secret weapon.

It didn't take us long to land eight monster snook, which weighed from 20 to 35 pounds. We'd caught our limit in record time; in fact, some were still kicking when we called it a day. After cranking the outboard just prior to leaving, we released our leftover shad. At which time we watched the snook attack them as they blew them up on top. Unintentionally, we had "live chummed" them.

Tom Mears has been a friend for years. In fact, every Christmas his wife insists on sending me one of her fabulous rum cakes. But when I asked Tom if he wanted to snook fish again, his answer caught me slightly off-guard.

"No thanks, Tom," he replied. "I'd rather quit as a winner, where my average snook weighs 25 pounds."

I guess you had to be there.

With lures, however, it's different. Take a scenario that unfolded in my own backyard when a spillway opened for the very first time. As you may have guessed, there's more to the story.

This egregious example of spillway overload took place near my home in Boca. The date of this gaffe' remains etched in my mind; since it was the day my sister got married. And guess who was supposed to be an usher, but who forgot all about it when the snook started hitting? I address my transgressions from a historical perspective.

As a teenager I'd fished the C-15 canal, a Water Management conduit that ties into Lake Ida–the largest inland lake in Delray Beach. And now C-15 was to gain a spillway, an event we "snook-heads" anxiously awaited. The purpose of spillways is to reduce inland flooding; an idea embraced by the general public. But for guys like me, it meant a whole lot more: big fish with stripes on their sides. I could feel the excitement build.

C-15 divides Boca Raton and Delray Beach, before emptying into the Intracoastal, just east of Federal Highway. We knew it was loaded with snook, especially in view of recent developments. Like when run-off started spilling over the newly-built dam and snook were seen feeding in the tailrace. They were busting on top, like jacks or bluefish, so we had little doubt what lay in store: When the gates opened, it would be a bloodbath. Thankfully, I had plenty of plugs.

I was working at Boca Tackle, and we'd just received a shipment of Bagley Bang-O-Lures: a wobbling plug that resembles a Rapala (which were hard to come-by at the time), as did several others of the same era. I remember it being the 12th of June, 1965–a date that will forever live "in family."

I expected a crowd for the opening. It would be a formal event with speeches and what-not, so I planned to get there early; armed with 12-pound spinning gear and a box of Bag-O-Lures. I'd use whatever I needed and pay for them later.

It was well-past midnight when I arrived at the spillway to find that I wasn't alone. Several anglers, who had gotten there before me, were already positioned below the flood gates, which were open and running–from the bottom up, in typical fashion. The current was seething and fish were feeding, visibly hitting on top. One gobbled my plug on the very first cast, and the rest, you could say, is history.

By daybreak, the crowd had grown to between 10 and 15 anglers, the majority of whom were busy fighting fish. It was mayhem incarnate for all concerned, while we cast and cranked like robots. As I watched the foam piling-up in the current, the occasional shad made it through unharmed. The snook, in the meantime, kept pressing their attack, from along both drop-offs to well below the dam. It made no difference where your lure landed. You had to pity those hapless shad.

They become disoriented in the fractured currents, and

probably forget which way is up. Meanwhile, more fishermen were getting the word, and they kept arriving in increasing numbers. They came armed with lures of every description, and in some cases, buckets of live bait. At a time when the limit was four snook apiece, the seawall resembled a food bank.

The majority of these fish weighed at least 10 pounds apiece, while some tipped the scales at more than 20. And all I could hear was shouting, as the mob scrambled from rock to rock. People tried not to stumble, but to no avail, and some ended-up in the drink. Like I said, it was mayhem.

I was hooking a fish on every cast, until my hands started to cramp. When I finally paused to glance at my watch, I discovered it was nearly noon. And I still had to shower and change my clothes. A few more casts and I'd leave, I promised.

There's a rhythm to fishing that numbs your senses. And speaking of sense, I forfeited mine the moment I hooked that first snook. I'd been fishing for 12 hours without a break, and from the looks of things, with no end in sight. I kept casting and reeling, and unhooking fish, oblivious to the watch on my wrist. If I hung it up now, I could make the reception. I promised to quit after two more snook.

If lies were nails, they'd seal my coffin. Was this a character flaw, or the world's worst manners? Could I ever make it up to my family? I'd been so caught-up in this free-for-all that the rest of the world had ceased to exist. Then once again, I lost track of time, until a look at the sky revealed a sunset. There'd be two more days like it in quick succession, and in-between, bouts of fitful sleep. Did the fish I was catching make it all worthwhile? Don't bother to ask my sister.

It was my custom in those days to only count snook that weighed 10 pounds or more apiece. And by the end of Day Three–not counting the small ones–I'd racked-up a total of 87, all on 12 pound-test spin or plug casting gear. Several of the larger ones weighed at least 30 pounds. When the slaughter subsided and I reached for my car door, I could barely hold onto the handle.

Nor could I stay awake in class the next day. And guess if I'd finished my homework? But in those happy times when you could "bribe" a teacher, I knew which of mine liked fish, as well as how much. You can call me a teacher's pet, but my test scores took a turn for the better. In fact, I referred to them henceforth as "spillway exams."

❖   ❖   ❖

Spillways, unquestionably, offer production-line fishing that has all the charm of a steel mill. But there's often a good chance of meat for the table, which frequently comes in an oversized package. You're surrounded by concrete and groaning metal, as the tongues of current run foaming and brown. Plus, you're typically standing on slippery rocks, while swill and flotsam lick at your feet.

But occasionally you find a silver lining, when more than just snook appear at a spillway. Take my late friend who met an attractive brunette, while of all things, she stood there casting a lure–and from what he told me, catching snook. A good-looking kid in his own right, he offered to lend a hand.

The upshot is that the pair started dating, and ended-up tying the knot. During their years together they visited exotic destinations, where snook were still on the menu (the sale of "domestic" snook has been prohibited in Florida for decades). Which brings up an interesting point.

I've enjoyed spectacular fishing during my years on the water, some of it thanks to spillways. These forbidding structures add a new dimension to what's already a multi-faceted sport. While the quest for fillets is what fueled my interest, spillways offer a great deal more. Perhaps their greatest contribution is teaching developing anglers to be ever mindful of changes: in the weather, the water and the fish.

Of course, catching 35-pound snook isn't all bad, either.

8

Mullet Miasma

"Tom fighting a tarpon during the mullet run
after it took all the line off his reel."

Photo by Mark Sosin.

The main event at South Florida beaches.

It begins as a trickle in a New Jersey marsh, before gaining momentum as it starts heading southward. By the time the main body reaches Sebastian Inlet, it resembles a living mat. If the mullet attract beachgoers, as well as game fish, it's because—in the words of one fisherman who looks forward to the run—"It's the greatest show on earth."

I can't think of a better description: Acres of baitfish heading south, while they're pummeled by predators of every description. It starts with the fall Nor'easters. After leaving estuaries as far north as New England, they work their way south along the Atlantic coast. When they finally arrive off Palm Beach County, where fishing access is readily available, they become the darlings of the local media. News crews in choppers then regale their audiences with the scenes of unfolding carnage.

At one time the schools were an endless ribbon that was constantly under attack. Although the runs have dwindled, there's still enough action to keep anglers busy for several weeks.

So what does this "mullet run" look like when all the conditions are right? Well, you'll see tarpon and snook joining jacks and sharks in a spray-filled arena where everything's hunted—with mullet at the bottom of the food chain. While the schools may extend several hundred yards offshore, the majority follow the surf line. Since lone fish are doomed, the mullet band together in schools that move as a unit. The schools tend to tighten when the attacks ramp-up, forcing some of the mullet's noses out of the water, while all around them the carnage rages.

It's an adrenaline rush for anglers like me, who watch the show from a few yards off. With a cast of characters that's virtually unequalled, it's the only one like it so close to shore. While snook and tarpon stand on their heads, phalanxes of jacks surf down the swells, and windrows of mullet take to the air. The effect resembles a slow-breaking snowball, as the schools explode from within. Of course, anyone foolish enough to swim in this mess takes their life in their hands.

❖   ❖   ❖

I'm reminded of a particular Sunday morning, and of sneaking away on my 10-speed bike. It was faster than the bus I was accustomed to taking, and it took me wherever I wanted to go. I saved the money to buy it by getting to work early and working extra hours. That bike, in return, brought the run within range, which lies at the heart of this "tail." Here's how it all got started:

I was expected in church that morning, but before donning clean pants and a neatly-pressed shirt, I slipped on a pair of bathing trunks. Then I headed for the Palmetto Park Pavilion, near some rocks where the mullet rested. That day, however, by the time I arrived the bait was moving, while predators raked it from every angle.

I parked my bike and stripped off my church clothes before stuffing them back in the handlebar basket—folded for the ride back home. Not bad, for a 14-year-old kid? But I forgot about the tide.

I was armed with my trusty Shakespeare rod and a Luxor "Seven Seas" spinning reel, the latter loaded with 12-pound mono—the blue stuff we used at the time. I'd attached a mono leader, along with a 7/0 hook, and beneath the hook, a tiny sinker. By casting my rig into a school, I could snag a mullet whenever I needed. I'd then drop it back to where I'd hooked it, and wait for a fish to hit. When the mullet were running, it didn't take long.

A few minutes later, I was high-tailing it south, chasing a jack that was "cleaning" my reel. As anyone who's caught one will probably agree, the really big ones lack a sense of humor. What they do have is strength and endurance. I was as short of breath as I was out of line.

The fight wore on for more than an hour, as I struggled to regain a few yards of line. I'd been walking for several miles, when there before me loomed Boca Inlet. The jack, in the meantime, kept heading south.

There was only one thing left to do—climb the jetty, then swim the inlet, and rejoin the fight on the opposite side. So with the bravado of youth, and no sense to speak of, I loosened my drag and grabbed the rod–between my teeth like a bird dog would. At which time I took the plunge.

I must have been an okay swimmer back then. Not to mention that since the mullet had yet to enter the inlet, there wasn't much risk involved—something I couldn't say for the surf. The current had slowed to a halt, making crossing the inlet quite a bit easier. Plus, when I finally arrived at the opposite jetty, several hands reached down and hoisted me up. By now, the jack had run far to the south.

I cleared my nose and ran for the beach in a last ditch effort to save my fish. Surprisingly, I recovered some line, something that so far I hadn't been able to do. The romp down the beach had me huffing and puffing, but I tried to back up whenever I could–before running forward and gaining a few turns. Line-stretch makes this difficult and the more you have out there, the tougher it gets. But the lopsided battle had taken a turn.

I could swallow the lump in my throat for a change, and see the Coast Guard helicopter that had been hovering off in the distance. And there beneath it were those mullet again—replete with the tarpon and sharks.

I kept making headway, and within the hour, I finally had the jack in the surf. It had dragged me to the Deerfield Pier, five miles from where the saga had begun. By now, we were both exhausted—my adversary, terminally so. So with the help of the waves, I managed to beach what was the largest jack I'd seen at the time: 43½ pounds on the scale at the pier, a catch I was proud of on 12-pound test line.

Now I had a different problem. I'd left my bike on Boca Beach, and I didn't look forward to hiking back, via A-1-A and the inlet bridge. So when a spectator offered to give me a lift, I jumped at the chance to accept.

By the time we arrived at the pavilion, a crowd had gathered and was milling around. I guessed that they'd come to admire my catch, currently in the trunk of the car. That was before I saw all the police cars, along with other official vehicles that I didn't recognize. Officers, apparently, were asking questions, and judging from their uniforms, they weren't from Boca. That sinking feeling returned again. Then, someone pointed me out.

The cops swooped in like a school of bluefish. I'd apparently been the object of an extensive manhunt that involved not only marine and land-based units, but also a Coast Guard chopper. You can guess which one by now, I'm sure. The authorities had been searching up and down the coast, since they didn't have a clue as to my whereabouts.

I'd been missing in action for nearly four hours. Then, when the tide came in it carried off my clothes (including the wallet I'd left in my pants). But when they all washed back, a swimmer found them and hurriedly called the authorities.

The presumption, I learned, was that I drowned while fishing, and that my body had drifted away—or that something more macabre had happened, based on the activity taking place in the surf. My bike, in the meantime, was right where I'd left it.

While I still had my share of explaining to do, my inquisitors were pleased with the outcome. Plus, they had yet to contact my mother—a blessing for which I'll be forever thankful.

While jacks may be fine for openers, they're not the featured performers—not during the mullet run. If there's a perennial star to these piscatorial pyrotechnics it's the "Silver King," or tarpon. So how do we locate these silvery giants? By driving along beach roads and staying alert.

You can't miss them feeding, when you know what to look for. In fact, everyone on the beach gets a front row seat, while they strafe the mullet in their relentless pursuit. The fish do back flips and explode through the schools, while they flash their sides at the flabbergasted crowds. There's no denying it's a lifeguard's nightmare, since any fish that size are mistaken for sharks.

The challenging part for my friends and me was finding a place to park. I'm referring specifically to Palm Beach Island, where exclusive properties line parts of the beach road. Then, don't forget our heavy gear, which made long walks that much less appealing, especially around high tide when the sand is softer. So the closer we got to the action, the better it boded for us.

Of course, there's always the matter of private property, which could mean anything above the high water mark. Once we reached the surf, we were never bothered. Maybe it's because we talked with the people and give away snook–usually to folks who worked in those mansions? That frequently led to us meeting the owners.

I recall one lovely lady asking her liveried butler to bring us glasses of iced tea and water—each with a slice of lemon. Then, once I enjoyed a ride in a limo, along with my four fish limit, back up the road to where I'd parked my car. Some homeowners offered us parking privileges, but we preferred to drop-off one car, then race off in the direction from which the fish were coming—meaning north. That ensured us a ride when were worn out from chasing fish.

Palm Beach, like I said, was a world apart, where tradition and courtesy were both part of the equation. The mullet, however, may have viewed it differently, since when they first came streaming from Palm Beach Inlet—where the schools went on the incoming tide—they faced an onslaught of unparalleled magnitude, and not just from snook and jacks. On several occasions, I dodged skyrocketing kingfish that literally cleared the jetty. I've even seen sailfish swim through the schools when the runs entered the inlet.

We'd intercept the run from the long south jetty, where the mayhem typically focused. It's also where locals, known as "Jetty Conchs", made some remarkable catches from the slippery rocks. Jetty fishing has its ups and downs, especially when you move around a lot—a process we facilitated by screwing bottle caps to the leather soles of our shoes, before covering them with pairs of woolen socks. We tried to maintain our balance, but failed more than once.

While snook (or even jacks) were our usual targets, huge tarpon also entered the mix. Feeding snook draw a crowd, and wherever that happens, mishaps are bound to occur. While the gear we used caused us minor injuries, it was nothing compared to a lightning bolt that struck the south jetty from out of the blue. I remember watching several fishermen rise to their feet again, and one that wasn't so lucky. It was hardly my only brush with lightning, as you'll read in another chapter.

Remember our heavy gear? Well, sometimes it bit you back. A perfect example took place one day while we were busy catching snook. We fished the jetty like we did the surf, except that here our tackle was even beefier. That's because we were often forced to "flip" our fish, like crewmen on a tuna boat. So while most of us fished with mid-size reels—say Penn "Squidders" and "Jigmasters"—we'd spool them with 80-pound test Ande mono. We'd snag a mullet and let it sink, and wait for that tell-tale "thump."

That's the way it was supposed to work. I once set the hook on what I thought was a snook, and out comes a 150-pound tarpon–that starts grey hounding across the inlet. My drag was locked, as you might have guessed, and I remember losing my footing. Then the next thing I knew, I was swallowing salt.

I held on for dear life while the fish kept running, although I finally managed to back off my drag. But by then I was 50 yards out in the inlet and caught in the outgoing tide. Still, I refused to let go of my rod, as at a time when possessions shouldn't have mattered. Meanwhile, the mullet were jumping all around me as unseen assailants ripped through their ranks. The current was strong—too strong to fight–and I felt myself running out of options. I was bobbing like a waterlogged coconut.

Then, just when I figured my luck had run out, some guy on a yacht snatched me out of the drink and dragged me into his cockpit. The tarpon had long since broken-off, but I still held onto my rod. A favorite outfit is like a horse to a cowboy, or so it seemed at the time. The man then motored to a nearby beach where he proceeded to drop me off. It wasn't that far from the jetty. Me? I was glad to be on solid ground again, although I was still shook-up by what had happened.

You need to understand the following in order to fully grasp the significance of my rescue: We jetty fishermen were forced to compete with huge sport fishing yachts that backed over our lines whenever they saw us catching fish. They'd end up dodging insults and sinkers, a formality that assured there was no love lost between us. But this Good Samaritan took the time to save me—for which I am grateful. Thanks, again, whoever you are.

Palm Beach Inlet was just the tip of the iceberg. Drive south several miles and you'll come to a curve, where at one time you'd pass Mar-A-Lago, socialite Marjorie Meriwether Post's castle by the sea. The current owner divided the estate, but back in those days we could park on the shoulder and hike to the beach. The world, like I said, was different then. In addition to visually searching for action, we relied on intelligence from the "Mullet Line."

What exactly was this Mullet Hot Line? Well, a dedicated number at Boca Tackle that our customers would call with specific information on the whereabouts of the migrating schools, along with what predators were dogging them, and how close they were to shore. Think of it as our crystal ball.

Let's say you were interested in snook. Well, we kept a chart that we updated daily from the call-in reports we received. We knew exactly when a school passed Lake Worth Pier–that they were mostly in the surf and that snook were harassing them. Similar reports kept tabs on tarpon—or anything else that was tracking the schools. It was like leading a covey of birds.

Speaking of tarpon, it was one such report that led to me picking the fight of my life. While most beach encounters play out the same, after you locate the mullet, I knew this one was going to be different. I couldn't believe the number of tarpon, as the mullet school passed the curve.

What's it like, an event of this magnitude? Well, you hike to wherever the tarpon appear concentrated; then all you can do is hope. One thing you count on is that you're bound to get wet— soaked to the bone by your hard-earned sweat.

I can still recall that day in detail: how I slogged along through the soft wet sand–my heart racing from that and the excitement–as mullet were forced ashore at my feet. Still, I hadn't reached where even more fish were showing, a hundred yards down the beach.

When I finally arrived there, I saw the six-foot flashes as sub-surface ruptures became full-blown explosions. Dozens of tarpon were airborne at once. I could literally taste the excitement. The weak of heart should avoid these scenarios.

I looked out to sea at that rippling mass, as the tarpon corralled the school. First, I'd snag a mullet on my single hook (over which I'd slipped a several-ounce bank sinker) before reeling it in to re-hook it.

So I did just that and removed the lead, before hooking it behind the dorsal. Then I tossed it out beyond the edge of the school, where multiple tarpon were rolling at once. By adjusting the tension, I controlled where it swam.

The hit came a moment later. It's hard to describe the visual effect when a tarpon that size vacuums the surface. I set back hard when the line came tight.

It was like hitting a solid brick wall, except that this wall kept picking up speed. The fish ran off over half my line before ever attempting to jump. When it did, I could barely believe it. Something else that made this fish so special: I was using 30-pound test, instead of my typical beach rig.

I'd come straight from the Lake Worth Pier, where we all used lighter line, after hearing about these fish on the Mullet Hot Line. They'd cleared Palm Beach Inlet the previous afternoon, so I knew right away where to look.

The battle teetered back and forth. First, I'd gain a few yards then the fish took it back. During much of the fight I could see my spool, but to add further drama would be redundant. Remember the jack at the start of this chapter? I now faced a similar hurdle—in the form of the near-shore drop-off.

Back in the days before beaches were "re-nourished," the surf had less of a slope. Meaning it dropped-off to a depth of four or five feet, depending on the stage of the tide. That extended the time required to subdue a big fish. The upshot of which was that this tarpon died.

Melancholy surrounded the carcass of this warrior who'd

given her all (the largest tarpon, remember, are females). The glazed expression, the smear of pink—results, no doubt, of some final effort—although the fish was hooked in the jaw latch. Neither angler nor fish had planned it that way. So I wrestled the tarpon back to my car with the help of several onlookers, before carting it off to the taxidermist.

The mount still hangs in my home. That fish tipped the scales at $187\frac{1}{2}$ pounds, although I wish she was still alive.

So where do the mullet go after making their run? That depends, I suppose, on who you ask. Some scientists believe that the run moves eastward, although we usually see the schools heading south—in the Intracoastal and on the beach–while plenty of mullet stay home every year. Then, every so often, you'll see a school offshore. There's also a run in the Gulf.

So maybe it's a pilgrimage of a different sort, where the schools disperse in the interest of survival. We fishermen suspect that it's not about spawning, since the tiniest migrants, known as "finger" mullet, are still too young to reproduce (at least, I've never seen one that carried eggs or milt). Some giants, in the meantime, yield gourmet roe.

So I'd like to think they reach Florida Bay, where they live out their lives in a state of grace. After running the gauntlet, I believe they deserve it.

Some days, I know how they feel.

9

The Wages of Sin

"Young angler Zane watches while his rod tip is replaced."

Photo by Matt Falvey.

Do fishermen learn to lie
(or are they born that way)?

My family wrote the book on being poor, so when we moved to Boca back in 1958, the only place we could afford to live in was a non-descript one room house. Seven siblings and I would share that house with our parents, without the benefit of surplus possessions. But my father–God bless him –figured at least we could fish. So he bought a few cane poles and a cheap rod and reel, which cost him $4.95 at the Piggly-Wiggly.

He would take us fishing on family outings, at which time we rotated the gear–with the caveat being that one of us would always get the rod and reel. I'd have it for 15 minutes or so before trading it off for a cane pole. But we'd only get it if Dad was there. Otherwise, we were told to leave it alone, and Dad meant what he said. However, parental pronouncements have extremely short shelf lives, especially in view of distractions.

Take the construction of the Boca Harbors subdivision, which included the digging of canals–the first such waterways to appear in Boca. At the time, I knew nothing about fishing the salt, nor did the rest of my family. So, on our outings to one favorite spot we'd bait our hooks with garden variety angleworms (which are considered a waste for salt water fishing). The canals where we fished still had no seawalls, and the banks were littered with freshly felled trees, a result of ongoing construction efforts. While my family set-up shop between the deadfalls, I took the rod and reel and went off to explore.

I hadn't gone far when I noticed a commotion, which decades later I understand. Apparently some jacks were chasing mullet when a baitfish made a run for shore and became trapped between the branches and the beach. I rushed down and grabbed it, before running back to my family–after placing my hook in its mouth. Then, I claimed I caught it on one of those worms. No excuses; it was a bold faced lie. And I'd just barely started fishing.

So are fishermen natural liars, or is it a trait they acquire through practice? It wasn't long afterwards that I received my comeuppance.

A few weeks later I was home alone when, once again, temptation reared its head. After re-discovering that combo in a closet, I "needed" to give it another try. So I snatched it up and burst out the door, and promptly managed to snap off the tip. You can bet I was scared to face my Dad, but fear alone wouldn't solve this problem. So I decided, instead, to shut my mouth and stash the outfit back in the closet.

Eventually, I told my sister, who had managed to save a few dollars that summer. Together, we hatched a plan. We unearthed the rod and hitch-hiked to a hardware store that sat on the corner of Federal Highway and Palmetto–five miles in each direction.

The owner replaced the tip in minutes. Then he charged me an appalling $1.75–nearly one third of the price of a brand new outfit. My sister had to lend me the money, or see me face Dad's wrath. Lucky for me, she came up with the cash.

I subsequently spent the next several weeks–day and night– collecting empty bottles that I redeemed for two-cents apiece. My efforts netted a total of four cases. It's the kind of lesson that sticks in your mind, but eventually I paid off the debt.

I'll never forget that shellacking–the one I received at the hardware store–at a time when I was still just a kid. What made matters worse was when I got my first job and discovered that tips cost 10-cents apiece.

I was 11 years old when I started working at Boca Tackle. But I've since made it a practice–wherever I worked–to give kids a discount on items like line, and always on rod and reel repairs. I figured if what happened to me was payback, it wouldn't hurt me to help foot the next kid's bill.

10

The Cutting Board
of Education

"Andy Bellisari holds a sail for Ms. Djuna."

Photo courtesy of Tom Greene.

Spare the rod and spoil the child?

A philosophical fisherman stated long ago that he "would not endeavor to make a man who is none, an angler by a book." To the credit of this Seventeenth Century sage, the best fishermen I know learned their skills through practice. It's a tale worth telling–especially, to do-it-yourselfers.

It was 1967, and my senior year at Boca High, when I was approached by a representative of Palm Beach County's Adult Education Program. Would I be interested, she asked me, in teaching a course–a free one on fishing that the County would pay me for? Those last magic words sealed the deal.

We met two nights a week in an elementary school classroom. Class sized varied between 20 and 35 students, since there weren't any attendance requirements per se. I started by teaching basic skills: bait-rigging, knot-tying, how to wrap leaders, before expanding the curriculum to include more advanced subjects, like how to throw a cast net–that sort of thing.

The money was okay, and the classes were fun. But the greatest benefit was making new contacts who would later become my friends. And come to think of it, there was something else.

We sold seafood where I worked at Boca Tackle, and you can guess who helped stock the cooler. So when the pompano were running in Boca Lake, I'd be there at daybreak with my surf rods and sand fleas. There were other fish, too, that I'd catch from shore that ended-up in our market. That's until I acquired a boat.

She wasn't much to look at. Just a lap strake hull powered by a 75 HP outboard that could make it through Boca Inlet, while keeping me dry in the process. But she was perfect for fishing the reef, which I'd do at night after leaving the shop. Snappers and groupers were big sellers at our market–which leads to an interesting sidebar.

I'd just gotten into work after my morning off, when the boss' wife mentioned a shipment–of grouper fillets from a local distributor. I'd been on Juno Pier all morning, where snook were hitting like gangbusters. I had four sets of fillets on ice in my truck, since according to law, they weren't allowed in the shop.

In Florida, it's illegal to sell, or possess, snook in a seafood market. And Boca Tackle definitely qualified. So I filleted what I caught on the lid of my cooler, and paid neighborhood kids to dispose of the carcasses at a boat ramp at the end of the street. Those kids, who knew me from hanging around, started picking-up tips on fishing. Now 30 years later, they still come around–only this time with kids of their own, who love fishing as much as they do.

But this time they come to Lighthouse Point, where I presently have a shop. It's a rite of passage that I see repeated, but back to the original story. . . .

When I went to inspect those "grouper" fillets, I smelled a rat. They weren't grouper at all, but snook. And who would know better than I, considering I just cleaned the ones in my cooler? I asked for the invoice and snatched-up the phone, and prepared to read someone the riot act.

I was in no mood for arguing, not with all that liability sitting out in plain sight. But whoever answered the phone said was there'd "been a mistake," and that "a driver was on the way." Someone had knowingly acquired those fillets–which coincided with all the illegal netting that was taking place off Blowing Rocks–20 miles north of Juno Pier.

People I knew had watched sein netters dragging snook by the hundreds onto the beach. Meanwhile, the fish we sold were legal–take snappers and groupers–which brings me back to the boat.

Summer's the time when our reef fishing peaks. It's also when the seas remain calm, in the absence of tropical cyclones. And since with Adult Education there's no time off, I had a ready-made crew that was willing to learn, while helping catch fish for our market.

The deal I came up with worked-out like this: Several of us would meet at the boat once a week–in addition to regular class. Then we'd head offshore and fish the reef. I'd provide gas, bait, and terminal tackle, while their job, essentially, was to bait-up and reel. When the trip was over, they'd clean-up the boat, while I gutted and iced-down the catch. I'd offer to cook-up some small fish for dinner, but my students just wanted to learn how to catch them. We continued this arrangement for three or four years.

You could call it my version of graduate school, where my more-advanced students got to hone their skills. The trips eventually became so popular that I had to raffle them off–literally. For one family in particular, they launched a career.

Enter Art and Andy Bellisari, a father-and-son who moved to Boca from Columbus, Ohio. Both attended my very first class–when Andy was 11 or 12 years old. Art fathered two sons after Andy, who like Art, played football for Ohio State–one at fullback and the other, at quarterback. They built a successful plumbing business, and purchased a Bertram–a 35-footer that Art named Proud Mary in honor of his wife, Mary Beth. I'll save the rest of the story for later.

Meanwhile, learning how to fish is a two-way street, where the instructor sometimes becomes the student. And there's no better tool for "hands-on" instruction than the fabled "Cuban Yo-Yo." I learned about yo-yo's, and a whole lot more, during impromptu sessions in the back of our shop, when Jim Smith, Allen Merritt, "Bolo John" Mumford and other legends stopped by to "shoot the breeze.". Whenever they held court, the stories would flow–which brings me back to the yo-yo.

I learned that Cuban market fishermen had used them for years–mostly for hand lining snappers. They're just wooden spools with a beveled edge that a hand liner casts like a spinning reel. While the Cubans carved theirs from wooden blocks, before sanding the edges to remove any splinters, ours were molded plastic: okay if you don't mind skipping tradition. Either is perfect for catching yellowtails, a snapper that responds well to small baits and light sinkers. So what's the deal about yo-yo's?

Well, you stay constantly in contact with your bait with this rig, since you're physically holding the line. And unlike with spinning or conventional gear, you literally "swim" hooked fish to the transom. Since there's limited sideways movement, you end-up with fewer tangles. At the end of the trip that means more fish in the box. Seafood has always been big in Cuba, where cattle are as scarce as custom-built tackle.

We also relied on regulation gear for everything from kingfish to mutton snappers. The latter which we fished for with 30-foot mono leaders that we baited with ballyhoo "plugs" (a dead ballyhoo with the tail cut-off). Since blankets of ballyhoo would swim through our night lights, we could cast net all we wanted.

Back when we made those weekly excursions, my students learned all about various types of tackle. As the weeks passed by, they became so proficient that they really started racking-up snappers. So whenever they hauled a nice one aboard, I'd yell out a number based on what the fish was worth–meaning at the market.

I'd say four bucks instead of four pounds: Can you remember when snapper was cheap? While you scratch your head, here's how we'd find them:

There's a reef in 60 feet of water, just north of Boca Inlet. The top, or crown, rises a good 15 feet before dropping-off along the reef's outer edge. We'd attempt to find it through triangulation–lining up objects on shore–before attempting to drop our anchor. Then we'd deploy our secret weapon.

That secret weapon was chum. We'd figure the current so that once we anchored, our slick would drift across as much reef as possible–in order to pull-in the maximum number of fish. So what did we use for chum? Better to ask what we didn't use.

At some point I learned about boiling egg noodles and mixing them with commercial blood chum, or with silversides or glass minnows–in a five-gallon bucket that we kept near the stern. That trick also works with boiled macaroni, as well as with crab shells and lobster heads. We'd collect anything a fish would possibly eat, then chop, grind, or pulverize it into usable form, before ladling it over the transom. Only then would we be ready to drift back our baits.

If I remember correctly, it was Barkey Garnsey who taught me the importance of sink rates–of having your bait and chum sink together. That's when the Cuban yo-yo is at its best, since you drop back your bait with minimal resistance, and with just enough weight to carry it down.

We did something similar with spinning gear, while trying to keep that in mind. If there's a central theme to what I learned from Barkey, it's that all great captains, and most good anglers, learned their craft by apprenticing on drift boats, or via some other on-the-job training. Which may have included a yo-yo.

Chumming is a god-send when fishing the reef, but occasionally it exhibits a sinister side. One of the best, or worst, stories I heard in that context was told to me by a customer. He rushed through the door of my store with one goal in mind: find a handle for his flying gaff. Then, still out of breath, he related the following:

He'd been fishing the reef with his elderly parents, when a commotion erupted alongside his Bertram—one of those 31-footers with the low freeboard. He was anchored and chumming for yellowtails at the time.

When he went to investigate, he discovered a mako (shark) trying to swallow his chum cage. While those cages are constructed from heavy-gauge wire, this shark didn't seem to mind. After ushering Mom and Pop up to the fly bridge, he searched the cabin for heavy tackle—something on which to bait the mako.

The best he could do was a 20-pound spin rig, hardly enough "gun" for the task at hand. But he'd he decided then and there to save his chum cage, regardless of the risk involved.

So he attached the line from his flying gaff hook to a cleat near the stern where the cage was hanging. Next, he rushed back inside, where try as he might, he still couldn't find the handle. He then returned to the cockpit with no time to spare.

The shark, he discovered, had been pressing its attack in an all-out effort to dislodge the cage. That's when he ran out of patience. There was something else, too.

He recalled that mako flesh was sought-after commodity, and

that it reminded some consumers of swordfish steaks. And this one already had its head out of water, and was practically in his cockpit.

So with no other recourse, he finally reacted by jamming the gaff hook into the monster's gills–something I wouldn't attempt on a bet. At which time the shark went ballistic. If you've ever seen a mako up-close–with those coal-black eyes and protruding teeth–just thinking about it gives you chills.

Meanwhile, all I could do was listen, frozen is disbelief.

The first thing I asked him then was: "Did it try to jump (makos are known for their spectacular leaps)? His answer?

"No, it dove straight for the bottom, while wrapping itself in the flying gaff line."

As I tried to visualize these events unfolding, he continued to tell the "tail."

Apparently, the mako became so entangled that it reeled itself back to the transom–where he gaffed it again with his regular pole gaff, before tying it off to a second line. He then immediately pulled anchor and dragged the shark backwards–all the way to Lighthouse Point Marina, just off the Intracoastal north of Hillsboro Inlet.

All I could think of was "yeah"–something I'm sure he sensed. But then he ran to his car, and returned with a photo.

And there he was with that mako, along with a sign that read "225 pounds" and "Lighthouse Point Marina."

I made tracks at once to my inner office, and found him a handle for that antique hook by raiding my personal collection.

Now he'll be ready the next time.

Speaking of Lighthouse Point Marina, that's where the Bellisari's kept their Bertram. And it's where we enjoyed some wonderful times, doing many of the things I've been talking about–sharing stories and trading techniques, while topping it off with great food and drink. Fast-forward two decades from my original class, to a time when the Bellisari's were first-class anglers.

Remember me mentioning their second career? Well, at one time we filmed a TV series, but I'll save the details for another time. We continued to make those afternoon trips, only this time in style and comfort with a depth recorder and live well, to boot. But now for additional background:

We South Floridians enjoy great offshore fishing, with Atlantic sailfish drawing the crowds. Since time immemorial, these nomadic wanderers have passed through our waters on their seasonal migrations. Since they typically follow the offshore reefs, they're there in our own backyard.

While the season peaks during the winter, some sails are "out there" all year long. You can see their sails as they surf down the swells, with the upper lobes of their tails exposed. Every town has a "Sailfish Alley," most of which roughly parallel the coastline in from 120 to 130 feet of water. The stretch from Hillsboro Inlet to Boynton Beach is no exception.

For reasons that should be obvious, everyone wants to catch one–a premise underscored by the number of mounts that have festooned marinas since the 1950's. Back in the days before catch-and-release, it was "put 'em on the dock." Mounts were big then, and probably still are, but anglers now purchase replica versions, which conform to the measurements of any fish they release. This precludes the need to bring back a carcass, which is a giant step for conservation. But getting back to the Bellisari's...

We enjoy a good sailfish bite both early and late, when most South Floridians aren't trapped at work. And we took advantage of it with the Bellisari's, who were always willing to lend a hand. We'd invite people who had never caught a sail, and race offshore to where the fish were waiting. After filling our well with live ballyhoo, we'd slow-troll them beyond the reef.

There's no better bait for sails. We'd catch ours either one at a time—on #12 hooks that we baited with tiny pieces of shrimp or squid—or in industrial-sized quantities by throwing a cast net, after lowering that familiar chum bag. Chum helps in catching ballyhoo, just as it does with yellowtail.

It wasn't unusual to land three to five sails during the last few hours of daylight. We'd fish north to Boca Inlet, where the water was bluer and we guessed, a lot saltier, and frequently deal with multiple hook-ups. The fish were so thick that, on several occasions, they became entangled in our lines.

Perhaps the greatest mystery unraveled so-to-speak, when a fish we'd "hooked" turned-out to be lassoed. It had managed to swim through the "legs" of a double line—just below the Bimini Twist. Sailfish may have been our major target, but they weren't our only prize.

While Art "bumped" the Bertram in and out of gear, with our surface lines in the outrigger clips, we'd also drop down weighted live baits: a move that led to the famous fish fries that we typically held on the marina dock. All it took was a radio message, and our friends would be waiting when we returned with mutton snapper iced-down in the fish box and sailfish release flags flying aloft. They, in return, would supply the beer.

This story hasn't changed since I lived it. And the best part is that it never will. As each generation gives way to another, we pass along our wisdom. And so it is with fishing:

Who could forget all those fabulous fish fries and Art Bellisari's grandchildren—in fact, the faces of all those wide-eyed kids? Now Andy is a full-time sport fishing captain, who wins tournaments here and in the Bahamas. If you recall, he was there at my very first class.

I see experienced anglers as keepers of the flame, hereditary instructors of an age-old craft. Those fish fries we enjoyed were the ultimate pay-off. While we sat back and enjoyed the fruits of our labors, the young folks would listen and soak it all in.

When they weren't jumping off the dock or feeding the pelicans.

11

Star Power

"Sam Snead unhooks a largemouth bass that he
caught from a pond on the Augusta Golf Course."

Sammy, we hardly knew ye

Some honest-to-goodness characters show up in tackle shops, and I've been privileged to have known a few. One that immediately comes to mind is a pro golf icon who wowed the crowds for most of his adult life. Allow me to introduce you to the legendary Sam Snead.

I first met Sam back when the Boca Hotel and Club was the social hub south of Palm Beach. Wealthy tourists would spend the winters there or commute back and forth via airline or train. These privileged few included a surplus of golfers who passed their time on the links or playing cards—gin rummy being a favorite. Some, like Sam, also fished. Back in those days there was no Senior Tour, although Snead won his last title at age 52 at the Greater Greensboro Open.

At the time, I was working at Boca Tackle, which was within walking distance of the pink hotel. Sam waltzed in one day just to "shoot the breeze" with anyone who was familiar with the local fishing. He'd been staying at the Club and had seen snook in the dock lights, and he claimed to have fished for bass in Kentucky, or wherever it was that he spent his summers. I figured what he needed was a guide like me who'd help him fish from his boat: a lap strake Chris-Craft with a 50-horse outboard that he hauled around on a trailer.

He knew he found his man when I mentioned bass. Well, almost a man, with me still in high school. But what did that matter, when it came to fishing? Besides, largemouth bass were one of my specialties.

Sam offered to pay me to guide him at Loxahatchee, a several-thousand acre wetland located west of Boca. That meant $35 a trip, which was nothing to sneeze at, compared to the $1.10 an hour I was earning at the shop. As an added bonus, I'd get to fish. This was an opportunity, to say the least.

In the 1960's, the road to the launch ramp was paved with gravel, which made for a bumpy ride. Snead, who was already in his early 50's, drove a "Woody" like the ones that were popular with surfers. Woodies hit the streets during the Second World War due to a shortage of metal. Meanwhile, Loxahatchee, which was part of the Everglades, included acres of wetlands and swamps.

Ducks, coots, and the ubiquitous gators filled a void that reached beyond the horizon. And tying it all together, like grid lines on a map, were canals and ditches that drained the marsh—some interrupted by spillways.

Sam's first real encounter with a South Florida marsh was announced by a slap on the chest, literally. We'd been running along the east/west canal when we discovered an opening where the waterway widened. It led to an expanse of shallow flats—and flats in general harbor larger bass, especially in the shelter of cat-tails. Here, every hundred yards for as far as we could see, cattails peppered the shallows. But, since 14 inches was too shallow to run in, we were forced to get out of the boat and push.

We had nearly arrived at the closest bunch, when a bass jumped up and hit Sam in the chest before falling into the boat. Sam instantly started screaming and turned pale as a ghost before he realized that it wasn't a snake. That bass, I might add, weighed five or six pounds. It happens in heavy cover.

When we fished the flats, we'd drift and cast until, hopefully, we found a deep spot. Maybe "trough" is a better word? Then we'd follow the trough to the east/west levee where eventually we'd find a spillway. If the spillway was running, so were the bass.

Those fish were typical "schoolies," one to three-pounders that fed on forage that was swept through the sluice with the current. We used Johnny O'Neil "Weed-Wings" and "Golly-Womper" worms. On a good day we'd catch between 30 and 40. But sometimes we stayed out in deeper water. Another favor-ite lure was a plug called the "Creek Chub Darter." That one sported two sets of trebles.

This leads to an interesting sidebar: when school bass are hungry they relinquish all caution. In fact, it's not that unusual to catch two at a time impaled on a single plug. Sam, however, expanded on the theory by landing two and claiming a third—that apparently worked free while being reeled to the boat.

I've never personally witnessed a triple, although I'd landed doubles before on numerous occasions—with bass, bluefish,

snook, and jacks. And come to think of it, with peacocks in Brazil. But three at a time? Then, I've never seen anyone hit a golf
ball like Sam.

I recall sunsets in the marsh, and how the shadows length-
ened while a mist started rising, like steam from the tepid swill.
The sounds we heard when the wind quit were more like a gentle buzz. This idyllic scenario had a well-worn texture, but one
trip stands out from all the rest: Sam's "one more cast" after we
should have left.

You play "long" when you're driving a golf ball, so why not do
it with fishing tackle—in Sam's case, a fiberglass Sila-Flex spinning rod and a Mitchell 300 reel? We were drifting along while
the sun sank lower, when Sam uncorked a "drive" that landed
beyond some cattails—where he had little, if any control. As the
slack kept falling, a monster bass, one of the grandest I'd seen in
the marsh, jumped up and grabbed his lure. Sam immediately
started jerking in an attempt to horse it before it became entangled in the vegetation, at which time it dove through the cattails.

I tried to keep him from breaking the line, but his ears were as
closed as the bail on his reel. He'd come unglued after seeing the
size of that bass when it jumped. While the drama unfolded, we
kept drifting closer, but there was no escaping what was about
to happen. So I went over the side in six feet of water, without
bothering to empty my pockets. With his line in one hand and my
other one free, I reached the cattails with only seconds to spare.

I'm not what you'd call an Olympic swimmer, but I dove
through the gloom and found that bass, wrapped in the reeds

with Sam's 12-pound line, just as I ran out of air.

I thrust my thumb in the fish's mouth, and pinched as hard as I could. By that time I had landed plenty of snook, so I knew how to handle a fish. Plus, Sam's hooks were singles, not trebles, so I didn't worry about getting pinned to the reeds. The bass, in the meantime, refused to stop struggling

I surfaced, all soaked and sputtering, and had to gasp for air before finding the energy to hoist that bass aloft. Sam, in the meantime, was sitting on the gunwales, wearing a crestfallen look. Apparently, he'd broken his line.

What followed could be compared to a resurrection, as Sam jumped up and started waving his arms. When I finally made it back to the boat, he reminded me how he had single-handedly landed that fish, as I dumped it on the deck. I was too worn-out at first to climb in. And when I finally did, I just lay there retching. Meanwhile, Sam was grinning from ear to ear like he'd just hit a double-eagle.

If my memory serves me, that bass weighed somewhere in the neighborhood of 12 pounds. I heard Sam carried its picture for the rest of his life, and that he'd tell anyone who'd listen about how he caught it. I wondered if they got the entire story.

We fished together at least 20 times, and he came into the shop several hundred more. I knew him so well that I made him a wager. Sam had offered to teach me to golf, but in those days I saw golf as a rich man's sport, and my family was as poor as

a church mouse. Then, I was much more interested in playing baseball, which I did for my high school team. That's how the wager got started.

I bet Sam I could hit a golf ball farther with my bat than he could with one of his clubs. If he won the bet, he would fish for free on our next outing; if he lost, he would pay me double. We agreed to meet after school at a driving range.

The outcome of that bet is etched in my mind, since it taught me a valuable lesson. My warm-up began with a bucket of balls and Sam's suggestion to, "Hit a few, kid." Some balls I hit made it past the 200 yard mark.

Then Sam stepped up with his custom golf bag, from which he withdrew a driver and then shoved a tee in the ground. By this time a crowd had gathered. The more balls I whacked, the larger it grew.

But now it was Sam's turn to address a ball. He asked the crowd if they'd judge the contest—to which they gladly agreed. He then walloped that ball with his classic swing, and it took-off for parts unknown. After 100 yards, it started rising, before turning to the left with the slightest draw. It eventually fell back on a lush patch of grass and proceeded to roll out of sight.

To put it mildly, the crowd went wild. Our next fishing trip was on me.

Wagers like that one weren't new to Sam. One of his favorite pastimes was to golf with the hotel guests, but only if they'd bet him a minimum of $100 per round. He gave out big handicaps, so sometimes they beat him.

When he lost, he'd pay-up with giant checks that he carried around in his golf bag. They read, "For beating Sam Snead in a golf match." Those checks, which were suitable for framing, were also legal tender. Of course, no one bothered to cash theirs. If anyone has one today, I'll bet it's worth plenty to the right collector.

Looking back on the years that I guided Sam, and the times we spoke in the shop, I may have enjoyed more "face time" with this sporting icon than anyone outside the Pro Tour. While I was just "a kid" at the time, I knew his opinion of other golfers, national politics, and just about everything else. I'd have to say that I came to respect him. Not only was he talented, but good-natured, too. He gave as much good as he got.

Maybe that's what sets a star apart?

12

Bassin', Profoundly

"My favorite bass trip took place several years later."
The bass in the photo weighed nearly 14 pounds
and was released back into the lake alive.

Games are what you make of them.

If necessity is the mother of invention, then imitation must be related, too. It's what got me involved with "America's Fish," the one-and-only largemouth bass. I morphed from a kid with a hook and bobber to a full-fledged competitor who was poised on the brink. Our relationship, however, was tenuous at best and the competitive part, short lived.

By the 1970's, I was hooked on snook: on piers, on bridges, at the inlets, and in the surf. It takes motivation to "bring home the bacon," especially with enigmatic species like the line-sider. For me, I needed to feed my family. Of course, nothing tastes better than freshly-caught snook, if it's not from too large a fish. But getting back to those freshwater "green groupers," and how fishing for one can lead to the other.

But first, a bit of background: Bass, like snook, can get awfully persnickety and occasionally suffer from lockjaw. Plus, the trophy specimens have minds of their own and they're often reclusive, to boot. Yet both share a predilection for outsized forage, while the smaller individuals fall for production-line techniques, not the least of which is chumming. So how did I make the connection?

Among the earliest venues where I learned how to fish was a series of local spillways. These concrete sluices that drain the suburbs are fountains of forage, as well as game fish. When summer rains cause canals to rise, ones in the suburbs fill to overflowing. This run-off teems with assorted prey: bluegills, threadfins, mollies, and shiners. Then, as now, it's shunted through conduits, which eventually lead to a spillway.

The clouds gather and the thunder rumbles before a summer deluge begins in earnest. Then later, while the downpour abates, steel screws turn, the gates lift, and the flood of forage sweeps into the salt. Snook, in turn, gather downstream in order to gorge on the glut. As this scenario unfolded, I'd sit and wait.

Frenzied feeding commences at the first sign of run-off, with threadfin shad the daily special. But since that wasn't always the case, I needed to catch whatever the snook were hitting in order to get my share. That meant cast nets and snag hooks, whatever it took.

This changing menu taught me to think independently, and led to my trying salt water techniques. I learned, for example, to catch fat "red" shiners that I'd chum like the ballyhoo we fished offshore, only this time I did it with bread balls.

And guess where I learned to catch wild shiners (say "freshwater lake" for an "A" in the course). Since shiners are effective for bass, it was only a matter of time. I'd brought the salt methods to lakes, while learning a trick or two in the process.

Lake Ida's the largest lake in Delray Beach, and it's visible from the local Interstate (one arm passes under the highway). The lake is loaded with shiners, along with threadfin shad and other forage. Rampant fertility makes for outstanding fishing, especially for trophy largemouths.

So along comes Tom Ryan, who lived in Delray and who's wrestling with a midlife crisis. He had been working in the audio/visual department at Florida Atlantic University while yearning for something "less-traditional." Or let's say he wanted to trade his office job for more time in the Great Outdoors.

Tom had been fishing at night and on weekends—the "bug" had bit him bad. His wife was a success in the dental business, so if there was ever a good time to make the change it definitely had to be now.

I suggested he become a bass guide.

We had been fishing together for several years, catching snook from the seawalls and bridges. Then Tom decided to buy a boat. With his local knowledge and my years of experience we began working together as a team. It was the perfect fit; I'd get a chance to do more fishing, using tricks I learned in the salt. And Tom would see whether they worked or not.

The typical approach to fishing a lake is to scour the shallows for cover. That usually means fishing the shoreline, but Lake Ida is surrounded by mansions and seawalls, and the shallows are literally clogged with weeds. The closest thing to a weed-free stretch was the approach to the water ski jump, which was located in the middle of the lake. All the constant boat traffic had mowed a trench. However, if I could attract any bass there, say by chumming, it would be a great place for us to fish.

For the next few months, we'd launch at daybreak and look for threadfins–armed with a six-foot cast net. They showed-up clearly on Tom's depth recorder. Mesh size was critical: anything larger than 3/8th-inch let the threadfins escape, but if the mesh was too small, it "gilled" and killed them.

Then we'd drift along the approach to the ski jump, sur-rounded by nothing but water. But as soon as we tossed out a few scoops of threadfins, bass started exploding all around us. They reacted like jacks or snook, which successfully proved our theory. Free-lining a live threadfin in the midst of this melee guaranteed action for an hour or two.

But the bass were smallish, and as the sun kept rising (or if skiers arrived ahead of schedule), the action slowed to a halt. After catching and releasing between twenty and thirty bass, we'd move on and search more traditional haunts, like under bridges that crossed arms of the lake, or along any shady shore-line. Remember that Interstate bridge I mentioned? It crosses a part of Ida known as C-15, which is actually a South Florida Water Management canal

That's where another friend, Tom Williams, caught a 13 ½-pounder on a rod he'd picked up less than two hours earlier. I built the rod for Williams myself. So, when he returned to the shop with his outfit in hand, my initial reaction was: "Don't tell me you broke it?"

"Not exactly," he said, before walking to his car and returning with one of the largest bass I've ever seen—caught on a plastic worm. We weighed it on the scale in the shop.

A third venue we fished was Lake Eden, also contiguous to Ida. But Eden, in contrast, was deeper than Ida, and the bottom was littered with rubble. That made it an ideal refuge for larger bass. We solved the problem of getting our baits down by adding a sinker, like we did offshore, to the terminal loop on a five-foot leader. We'd affix a snap-swivel to our main line, so we could change the weight at will. This allowed us to fish at different depths.

So how did we fish those arms of the lake that were typically bathed in shadow? By slow-trolling live shiners–which we rigged behind worm leads that we'd change according to the depth— along the banks It was like fishing for sailfish offshore, with one line short and the other one long (meaning back 100 feet or more). When a shiner got nervous, it ran to the top where the other angler would try to "steal" the action by reeling his bait to the strike zone, all in good natured fun.

Trolling live shiners was highly-effective, and just the ticket for trophy largemouths. Some clients simply liked catching the bait (which measured as much as 12 inches long), while others insisted on casting lures. Fishing in residential canals occasionally led to conflicts when residents saw their "pets" being caught–by strangers literally in their own backyards. And Ryan had learned how to rack-up the numbers.

Always the gentleman, he defused these situations by releasing the fish in view of whoever was watching. But before letting them go, he'd measure them first, before taking a snapshot or two.

You'll read more about it later in this chapter. For now, take my word that it all worked out, including for the bass.

Ryan's record numbers sound incredible today, since those bass were caught in the suburbs. But I have the photos to prove it. Take when Joe Munson and I landed eight or nine monsters that weighed 8 pounds or more during a single outing—the first time I showed Ryan my sinker technique. Or on my very first date with my wife-to-be, when she caught eight giant bass to my three. Once again, while fishing with Ryan. Who told you that life is fair? She claims to this day that it was all in her perfume.

Salt water tactics paid off for Ryan, who always remained a "crossover" fan. When the bass weren't hitting in Ida, he'd trailer his skiff up I-95, before launching in the Lake Worth Lagoon. This natural waterway forms the boundary between the mainland and Palm Beach Island. After running south in the "Lake," he'd fish in the shadows of West Palm Beach, where school fish swarmed during the winter months—salt water predators we know as "crowd-pleasers."

The stretch between Flagler and Southern Boulevard bridges would be overrun by the "poor man's tarpon"-more-correctly, the ladyfish or chiro. These dervishes run and jump like a much larger fish (a four-pounder is considered trophy material) and seldom failed to delight. Bluefish and pompano also obliged for anyone fishing a jig tipped with shrimp. Plus, some really big jacks waited in the wings.

If there's a moral to Ryan, it's this: He kept a legion of customers catching and happy, and it all started out with bass. His dark-green skiff, the *Guiding Light* was a local fixture for more than a decade. If a credo defines his successful career, it's that he was always willing to try new techniques, including the ones we learned in the salt.

Now, there comes a time in a bassin' man's life when he decides to go for the gusto. And who among us hasn't been tempted? We've heard of the fortunes that bass pros earn, but some of us aren't aware of the downside—that the road to success is paved with pitfalls, as the following hopefully illustrates.

I met Chuck Fairmont in my Lighthouse Point store and we started talking about bass. He owned a string of restaurants, so he had plenty of money to pursue the trophies. Yet he'd never landed one of five pounds or more, so I offered to lend a hand.

"I can get you a five pounder tomorrow morning. We'll be back at the shop before noon," I said.

He accepted my offer and I kept my promise, which led to a lasting friendship. As you probably guessed, I took him to Ida.

After such a rousing introduction, Chuck purchased a bass boat that was strictly state-of-the-art. It was a Storm, which was all the rage at the time. Eventually, he fished the Professional Tour, after entering local tournaments with his friend, Dale Flickenger—my snook fishing mentor from the Camino Real Bridge.

When Chuck decided to pursue greater rewards, he was kind enough to invite me along. It was to a Ray Scott tournament on Lake Okeechobee. Chuck agreed to show me the ropes (we call it "pre-fishing") for two days running before the contest started; then I'd be on my own. In "draw" tournaments like this, entrants without boats are paired with those who do. Then we fish together as partners. No one learns their partner's identity until at dinner before the next day's fishing. This was my one and only major tournament, and all I knew was how to catch bass.

At the opening festivities, I was approached by a guy who must have stood all of six-feet five. I remember him wearing a jumpsuit and someone saying he hailed from Arkansas. "You Tom Greene?" he asked me flatly. Then, "We leave the dock at 5:45 a.m. If you're not on time, I'm leaving without you."

No small talk or friendly exchange. Not even so much as a "pleased to meet you." He was as cut-and-dry as they come.

I stood on the dock at the appointed hour when I heard him bellow from the deck of his boat, "Well, are you coming or not?" We left the marina without saying a word and set off across the lake.

I hunkered as far down in down in my seat as I could, while trying to hold my rods–along with a small plastic tackle box. Meanwhile, all his gear was strapped to the deck. It was a ride to remember, to say the least, during which we may have broken the sound barrier (maybe that's why he had nothing to say).

We finally arrived at a part of the lake that the locals refer to as the "Monkey Box." He had already dropped the trolling motor and started casting by the time I finished rigging my rod. I watched as he skipped several bass to the boat, which he subsequently dropped in his live-well. Each competitor gets his own to use, and it's strictly off limits to anyone else. None of his fish amounted to much.

I stood in the stern, so I had the advantage, while he maneuvered the boat from the bow. Meanwhile, by casting my worm onto floating weed beds, then pulling it off and letting it drop, I was hooking a fish on practically every cast. And mine were bigger than his.

My victory was destined to be short-lived

He began grumbling in his off-putting manner, making comments like, "How {did I} like having my own *&%%$ guide?"

It was time to switch positions.

Despite my lack of experience in bass boats (his trolling motor was one of those "new" foot pedal models) I kept it on course down a narrow channel that was bordered on both sides by weeds. I was still able to cover them from my new position, so as the day wore on, my numbers increased, along with the weight of my "stringer." It's customary for contestants to cull any smaller fish, while keeping their daily limit.

If you haven't fished a sanctioned tournament, the rules work something like this: Each night your limit is weighed at the dock— with the fish suspended in a water-filled container. That's so they won't be injured before they're released. Your total is known as your "stringer." The winner at the end of these three-day events is the angler with the heaviest total. Plus, there's also a prize for the heaviest fish.

Something like 150 anglers had registered here, but I could

tell already that I was holding my own, with a stringer that might put me into the running. Plus, my partner had changed his tune. All of a sudden, he started acting like we were the best of friends. In fact, he started using my worms and worm weights, and asking me questions about my technique. I couldn't believe my ears. That night at dinner, I met his replacement, an older gentleman who wasn't quite so serious. I guessed that he liked to hang out with the tour pros.

But he told me not to worry about finding fish, since his buddy had told him "where they were." I was just two ounces out of first place.

On day Number Two, we left before dawn, before heading to "his" spot in the middle of the lake. What I failed to comprehend—as if it made any difference—was that each of us was allowed to control the boat for half of each day. I already knew where the bass were hitting, having been there the day before. But he insisted on fishing the lily pads, out in the middle of nowhere.

After hours of boredom, I'd landed three or four small ones. The wind, in the meantime, continued to strengthen until we were facing gusts of gale force strength. So like cattail chaff in the howling Zephyr, we were drifting along when a "real" bass hit.

She gobbled my worm off the surface (bass that size are invariably females), as it skipped past a stand of cattails. I knew from the swirl and the dogged resistance that this was a potential winner. It was touch-and-go for several minutes, until after scrambling around on my hands and knees, I grabbed her jaw and hoisted her aboard.

When I stooped to lower her into the live-well, the bass that were in there came unglued. It happens when light interrupts the darkness, which is why modern bass boats feature lighted wells. Of course, all I saw was that monster fish.

Ten pounds, at least, I was sure. When I looked at my hands, they were visibly shaking.

That night when we arrived at the weigh-in, Ray Scott was basking in the media spotlight. Cameras flashed and loudspeakers blared, as Scott announced the current leaders. I heard him say, "Here comes Tom Greene, who only needs so-and-so to lead the pack."

I had that and more by a substantial margin—thanks to the fish in the well.

Apparently, no one had entered any worthwhile totals, and the big bass so far weighed less than eight pounds. So my heart was pounding and my mouth felt dry as we motored up to the dock. I stepped forward to hand off the bow line, while an official handed my partner the weighing tray.

The moment of truth had arrived, but things were about to turn for the worse.

When I heard the crowd scream, I turned around. And there on the deck was my bass, flopping wildly as it slid toward the edge. My partner had opened my live-well, something he wasn't permitted to do, and when he did—out jumped that fish.

I knocked him out of the way, and in a last-ditch effort, dove for the fish. But all I could do was touch its tail as it slipped over the side and into the drink. The crowd was literally dumb-struck.

All I could hear was a collective gasp.

That moment cost me $50,000, and changed my life in the blink of an eye. Tournament prizes include trucks and boats, and at the time, I earned $187.50 a week. I had arrived at a crossroads of conscience, but I made a decision that I haven't regretted. That night at dinner, I received condolences from people I hadn't met before. Apparently, I wasn't the first guy to suffer this fate.

But all I kept seeing was that fish on the deck—flopping beneath my frozen partner. So at 4 a.m.—with no hope of sleep—I packed-up my gear and headed home. I stopped somewhere at around 5 a.m. to inform the office of my intention to withdraw, which was the gentlemanly thing to do. My ranking at this point was either eighth or ninth.

I never fished competitively for bass again, although some of my friends and customers do. I have, however, built a successful business—one that's not based on the luck of the draw. I guess it depends on your goals, different strokes for different folks.

My favorite bass trip took place several years later.

My eight year-old son and his mother were spending the week at a place called Lake Placid. We had rented a home there that I hoped to buy, and she had invited me up for the weekend. I was stuck at work as usual, but I promised to get there after we closed. She had also invited my brothers and sisters, who all had kids of their own.

I had always imagined a home on a lake where I could teach the next generation how to swim and fish. So, when I finally left work, I packed up some gear, including several cane poles rigged with hooks and bobbers. I also took a rod and reel for each of my nephews. The kids, I figured, could fish for shiners.

As for me, I hadn't fished Lake Placid, or any freshwater body since Okeechobee. The last worm I used on that final day still hung on a guide on my rod. This wasn't a fishing trip, per se, but I had decided to bring that outfit along.

When I finally arrived and looked at the lake, I was tempted to throw in the towel. The water appeared clear and lifeless. In fact, we spent the next two days dunking bread balls and worms—and shiners I purchased at a local bait shop—without the hint of a bite.

But all that changed on Sunday evening.

Valentino, our golden retriever, scared off a snake, creating a ruckus. Then, once the excitement subsided, the kids returned to the water after tethering Valentino to a 50-foot retractable leash. Time, at last, to relax.

I took a walk to the end of the dock, where to my surprise, some shiners had gathered. Life at last! I couldn't believe it. But by the time I returned with the rods and reels, the shiners had disappeared. They were all I had seen in three days of looking. So, more from boredom than any hope of success, I let fly with that plastic worm—the last one I'd used on Okeechobee.

With shadows gathering and the full moon rising, I paused to reflect on the tranquil surroundings. So when my line came tight on the third or fourth cast, I figured I'd hit a snag. But a moment later, when the snag started moving, I instinctively changed my tune. I remembered the weed-choked shallows and instantly backed-off the drag. I wanted that fish to run and tire itself out in deeper water. I still wasn't sure what I'd hooked. But when I heard it splash some 50 yards out, I knew I'd made the right decision.

All at once, the kids came running. I kept up the pressure, and it was give-and-take, until 15 minutes later the fish rolled on its side. I'm not all that sure of the time, since I was barely able to see my wrist watch. But I was finally able to lie on my stomach and grab the fish by its lower jaw.

The first thing I asked for was Valentino's leash, and the kids ran as fast as they could to get it. I slipped the snap through the fish's gills, before hooking it back on the retractable cord. Then I lowered it back in the lake in order to revive it.

A few moments later I "caught" it again, only this time by reeling the leash. After grabbing its lip, I held it aloft where my wife snapped photos with two separate cameras. Here was a memory worth keeping.

The next thing I did was measure both length (36 inches, as I recall) and girth, against a "noodle"—a tubular floatation device that the kids had been using. Then I eased it back in the lake, where it righted itself and swam away.

Now, here's where the tale takes an interesting turn.

Bill Nahrstedt, my friend since we were in the fourth grade, had recently moved to Avon Park, where he operated a taxidermy studio. He's still there, at Bill's Authentic Fish Taxidermy.

Bill made it a practice to mount all the big bass that inadvertently died on the line. The local guides helped him out in this project by bringing him fish that their clients had gut-hooked, but that they hadn't cared to mount.

Since the local lakes were (and still are) full of trophies, Bill's inventory eventually grew. By this time, the guides could offer their clients an alternative to killing big fish for a mount. Say, a "sport" landed a once-in-a-lifetime catch, now the guide could measure its length and the girth, and (hopefully) shoot a photo, before returning the fish to the water. He would then directs his client to Bill, who probably had an identical match. It reduced the number of "wasted" fish. Plus, it precluded the need to kill the big spawners—a giant step for conservation.

Remember Tom Ryan and measuring those fish? Well, Ryan explained to his clients what Bill had to offer and sent the measurements directly to Bill: an idea whose time had come.

You can imagine Bill's role in my personal saga. I called immediately with measurements of my own to see if he had anything that matched my fish. He suggested I come by and look. So, the following morning I packed up the car and drove with the kids to Avon Park.

Bill's studio was a virtual museum that contained fish and birds of every description, along with deer and hogs in various poses. The kids, need I say, were duly impressed. And Bill had the perfect match. That fish, according to the formula still in use (length times girth squared, divided by 800), weighed somewhere between 13½ and 14 pounds. Not bad for a "placid" lake.

So is it true what the publicists say–about largemouth being "everyone's fish?" After all, the species is found in all the contiguous states, and thanks to stocking, in locations worldwide. As far as "everyone's fish," that's your call, but I'm inclined to agree with the likes of Ray Scott—the Bassin' Ambassador who made it possible.

When I pause to look back on my bassin' career (in bass circles, it's customary to drop the final consonant in words like bassin,' flippin,' rippin,' etc.), I see the many facets of a single fish. There's the pervasive influence of sponsored products that change as fast as the wind on a lake. But there's also homespun charm and the idyllic memories of Saturday mornings spent free-lining shiners or pitchin' worms.

Like everything else, you make what you want of it: serious endeavor or light-hearted fun. Me? I choose the latter.

13

Zapped

"Yet few things in this world will ever prepare you
for a jolt that comes from above."

Photo by Steve Kantner.

A primer on death from the sky.

Anyone who plans on doing much fishing should keep one thing in mind. You'll face rain, wind, and other annoyances, and learn the meaning of wet and cold. Hopefully, you'll stay warm and dry, and if that's not an option, there's protective clothing. Yet few things in this world will ever protect you for a jolt that comes from above.

I've heard it said that the West has its mountains, while Florida has the clouds. With those clouds comes lightning, which here in Florida claims more lives than either hurricanes or tornadoes. Call it Nature's Grim Reaper; in fact, a single bolt can send 1 billion volts surging into the ground or water. With temperatures approaching those of the sun, a lightning strike wields a double-edged sword. That's not an exciting prospect for those of us who spend much time outdoors.

So here's hoping that these "tails" alert you to the dangers of this mysterious but deadly phenomenon. Why do lightning deaths occur so often? Is it the result of poor judgment on the part of the victim? I'll let you decide for yourself.

163

It was early afternoon on Lake Worth Pier, and what remained of the fishing had assumed a rhythm. Cast a live pilchard or thread herring beyond the bait school and, occasionally, you'd get a hit–from a snook or bonito (okay, false albacore).

I was interested in snook, as is usually the case, having exhausted my patience on the bullish bonitos. Their major contribution on hot July days was stripping line from my reels.

As usual, the air was humid and still, and the temperature hovered in the low to mid-nineties. No relief was in sight because of a thunderhead that managed to block the breeze. The storm was approaching the pier from the west, but since it was moving so slowly, no one gave it much thought. We had yet to feel the downdraft, and any lightning we saw was miles away.

The snook eventually started to feed. In fact, my friends and I had put five on the deck (back when the limit was four apiece) when the light started to fade–as high clouds began filtering the sunlight. However, that was enough to perk-up the snook: fish that had drifted into dormancy as the sun rose higher. Soon we were hooking fish on every cast. Several of my friends were starting to free-line. Then, suddenly, time stood still.

The next thing I remember was lying flat on the deck, sprawled like a splintered doll. My eyes, although open, refused to focus, and all I could feel was a painful buzz. My heart, in the meantime, was pounding wildly.

I was unable to discern any sounds per se, although I vaguely recalled an explosion. When I attempted to move, my muscles refused. Plus, I distinctly recall something burning. Was I dead or alive? I wasn't quite sure. I had seen that fateful flash. It was like falling into the sun.

Eventually, the feeling returned to my arms and I was able to turn on my side. Don Caylor, my friend, lay on the deck beside me, his hair singed and standing on end. His expression was one of confusion. Like me, he could barely hear or speak.

I'd lost all sense of time. I remember the downpour beginning and cold rain against my skin. Somehow it seemed to quench the fire, as if I was hot to the touch. I knew I needed to make it to cover, but I still couldn't rise to my feet.

My memory, I could tell, was starting to return. I began suspecting what had happened, but had no idea of the severity or proximity of the strike. The panicked crowd that was fishing the "tee" jumped over our bodies as they raced for the shop. No one, I realized, had attempted to help us, but I was too numb to feel either anger or fear. Pain and weakness were other matters.

Minutes passed before I could rise to my feet, soaked by sheets of driving rain. I knew we needed to reach the shop, a distance of 300 yards, where shelter awaited us. Suddenly, the rain felt like pellets. The temperature had noticeably dropped.

We staggered at first, before picking up speed. Eventually, however, we were able to jog. The deck was soaked from the relentless downpour and coated with fish slime, as well. While lightning kept crackling all around us, thunder resounded in deafening claps. After an eternity, I burst through the shop door and discovered the others huddled and shivering.

They said things like, "We saw it hit, but we didn't know where" or "We were afraid to touch you." All the while, the storm raged-on.

Pier Master Bill Narsiff stood behind the counter, looking out through the jalousie windows. Even this implacable character had taken an interest in one of the worst storms we'd ever seen. On racks behind him hung rods and reels that belonged to members of Lake Worth's "Big Game Club." Then eventually the storm abated, after squandering its energy and heading offshore.

In its wake the silence was deafening. The first thing I recall after stepping outside was the bitter-sweet smell of creosote, the result of all the soaked wooden pilings. The sky was gray and the air, dead-still and both were laden with static and moisture. Then one of my friends voiced the obvious: "What about our tackle?"

We had tossed out live baits on several big rods, but as luck would have it, not our free-lining rigs. Since we were now able to run, we took off sprinting to where we had left our gear.

When we found it, everything seemed intact, except for our light rods which were scattered like toothpicks. Nothing was damaged, or so it appeared, until Don noticed his heavy rod. His immediate reaction: "Who cut my line?"

We glanced at each other, unable to answer, until somebody took a look at the tip. The line had been severed, just as Don insisted, while the actual rod blank had been blown to bits. All the guides had melted into non-descript blobs that resembled beads of solder. The mono had parted wherever it touched them, leaving sections between them to cling to the rod like strings of toothpaste. When Don hefted his reel, it was warm to the touch.

The gears and side plate were fused together – frozen in a rictus of molten plastic. Mono and spool now formed a unit. Plus, the heat had managed to warp the reel seat. Don's outfit was effectively trashed. What had happened now became all too clear.

I was standing next to that rod – two feet away at most – when the lightning struck it. Any closer and I would have fried (not been lightly toasted). I must not have leaned on the railing, or I might have exploded like Don's rod tip. As far as any warning, there hadn't been one.

When I made it home at the end of the day, my mother's reaction said it all. After taking one look, she immediately asked, "Are you all right?"

I wasn't quite sure what she meant at first. Then, when she asked me if I'd been in a fire, suddenly it all made sense. She'd seen what was left of my eyebrows and lashes, along with the hair on the back of my forearms. I swallowed the lump in my throat, remembering Don's rod and what was left of his reel. What hair I had left stood straight on end, while goose bumps covered my charbroiled forearms.

That storm, admittedly, had moved out to sea. But what would I do when the next one appeared? I hoped I would use better judgment, especially in light of another close call–on the south jetty at Palm Beach Inlet, where I saw a fisherman killed.

Apparently, two "passes" weren't enough, but the third time is often the charm.

My next close encounter was at Boynton Inlet, on the night of the full moon in June—a time I could count on for a limit of snook, regardless of the weather or other variables. I was there with Scott Hitch, another of my friends who was afflicted with "Snook Fishing Fever." When the tide started falling around 2 a.m., we made our way onto the short south jetty, armed with our rods and a cast net.

It's typical for mullet to exit an inlet at the start of the outgoing tide. However, that night pickings were slim. The water looked oily and lifeless. For the first hour or two we struggled to net bait, and between us, landed a single snook. We tried plugs and jigs, whatever it took, but had nothing to show for our efforts. Then suddenly everything changed.

Like magic, the mullet appeared in droves, swimming against the current. They were coming around the north jetty, like in the mullet run. It took no time at all for the snook to find them.

Snook started cart wheeling through the frenzied schools, which now filled the inlet from jetty to jetty. Then, at one point, we noticed the tiniest flicker set against faraway thunder. Summer storms appeared in the daytime; this was the dead of night.

The insanity continued to escalate. We were hooking snook on every cast. In fact, I'd empty my cast net onto the jetty, so we'd have mullet whenever we needed one. We'd cast our baits, rigged below heavy sinkers, slightly upstream to roll with the current. They'd barely hit bottom before a line-sider grabbed them.

The slaughter continued for more than an hour, as the storm kept creeping in from the west. Then, what started as a few scattered bolts quickly erupted into dozens. Our catch-and-releasing continued to quicken, while somehow we ignored all the warnings, including the lack of other anglers.

Plenty of folks fished that jetty for snook, people from all walks of life. It was the height of the season, yet we were all alone. The storm continued bearing down and lighting the sky, although it had yet to reach the jetty.

Scott and I stayed locked on the action until the storm arrived overhead. What made it more frightening was the lightning display that was now turning night into day. While the bolts kept firing, the snook went berserk; we had front row seats for either show.

As the strikes got closer, their frequency increased. It got so bad that boats out for kingfish or snapper began high-tailing it back through the inlet. When one bolt hit the north jetty, we could literally smell the ozone. Plus, we were burned by a cable railing that reacted to the surplus of airborne electrons. By now, we had gotten the message – escape the storm or forfeit our lives.

Running was futile; the storm was too close. All we could do now was climb into the rocks, which were giant boulders with jagged edges. We decided to leave our tackle behind. What could it matter now?

The surface of the jetty–which was flat–rested on massive boulders, between which spaces continued inward for 10 feet or more. That's where we attempted to crawl, although the crevices were cramped for two guys our size.

Yet crawl we did, all slimy and soaked, as the storm continued to rage around us. As each bolt hit, we would grit our teeth and try not to think of the possible outcome. What if a bolt struck the rocks above us, like it had across the inlet? At one point we suspected a really close call, when a shock reached us through the rocks. We were just plain scared by now.

The storm wouldn't pass, making matters worse, or grant us a moment's respite. So we lay there shivering in our cramped quarters, praying that this monster would eventually depart. Meanwhile, all we kept hearing was thunder, a deafening reminder of our precarious position. A hit nearby and we knew we'd get zapped.

It's not easy to remember how long we lay there, clenching our teeth as the fury raged. But eventually the flashes and thunder ceased. When we finally attempted to retrace our tracks, our limbs were too stiff to make much progress. It took will power and sweat to escape our prison.

As we neared the surface, a light appeared, but this time without any thunder. It occurred to us then we'd survived the storm.

Other fishermen, who had remained in the parking lot, were finally wandering onto the jetty. When they saw our tackle, yet no signs of life, they started to look around. It was only then, when they approached where we'd hidden, that they heard us groaning as we crawled from the rocks. A few climbed down to help us. It was one of their flashlights that we'd seen through the crevice.

The rest of that night went according to plan. The snook went ballistic again before daybreak. Then, however, we kept four or five, unlike all the ones we released.

If there's a lesson to be learned, it's simply this: Lightning is reluctant to take any prisoners, and if you hear the thunder, you're a potential target. We read the statistics; these tragedies make headlines. Plus, people get killed on sunny days by strikes that come from faraway clouds.

We were lucky then; we're wiser now.

14

Casting It Far and Wide

"Throwing a cast net in the surf at sunrise."

Photo by Jack Hutton, courtesy of Tom Greene.

A net full of brief (and not-so-brief) encounters.

Remember those old-time gladiator movies, where a guy a sword fights another with a trident, who just happens to be also toting a net? Well, that second guy symbolizes ol' King Neptune and the conflict, the clash between humans and fish.

I've used cast nets for years for catching my live bait, mostly without a hitch. But one thing I've learned is, like any tool, cast nets can only give back as good as they get. Take something I witnessed at Boynton Inlet.

If you've been there, you know the current; it's as close as we get here to a raging torrent. It propels mullet from the Intracoastal into the blue Atlantic with all the force of a fire hydrant (a metaphor I was destined to regret).

My friends and I were on the jetty, and getting ready to fish the outgoing tide. It was early fall, a time when everyone else was catching jacks and bluefish, while we waited to target the snook. Our bait of choice was a live mullet, which is why a few of us carried cast nets.

Meanwhile, the trick to "safe" netting in a heavy current lies in not being greedy or taking chances. Once loaded with mullet, especially large ones, a net can get caught up in the flow and drag you along with it. I've seen it happen on several occasions.

On the day in question, a giant of a man stood perched near the tip of the jetty, waiting for the mullet to pass. He had a 12 foot net, which holds hundreds of bait fish.

I attempted to strike up a conversation, while we scanned the current for a passing school. Foam tickled barnacle-clad boulders beneath my feet, as the plume of brown water pushed out to sea. These were no conditions for a neophyte. I noticed that he stood near a five gallon bucket, which I assumed he intended to fill-up with bait. The exchange that followed was short and not sweet.

"I'm not trying to mind your business, friend—but, if you load that big net with too many mullet, the current will take it and you along with it."

I'd learned how to throw and "tuck" a net, and also how one behaved in the current. One time, I threw mine too close to a spillway in an attempt to load-up on gizzard shad. It would have been my undoing if a bystander hadn't cut the rope.

But the guy on the jetty didn't want my advice, so I turned my back and walked away.

It was only later, when I heard him shouting, that I realized my prediction had come true. He'd been yanked off the jetty by a net full of mullet, which had glittered briefly before disappearing. The sea then swallowed both him and the net, and both remained submerged while the current took them.

Two off-duty firemen were there on the jetty, and they dove in and attempted to save him—something, regrettably, they were unable to do. The man subsequently drowned before anyone could find him.

Remember my metaphor about the fire hydrant? It was a horrific event that I'll never forget.

On other occasions, I've seen tragedy averted. Take once when a cast net caught a moving boat—one running at night with its lights turned off. It was back in the days when smuggling was rampant. Of course, the craft rushed full-tilt from under a bridge where someone was cast netting mullet. The boat had managed to spook some bait, but the netter didn't know its whereabouts until he'd launched his net. He ended-up "netting" the T-Top. Fortunately for him, the swivel broke and he wasn't seriously injured. The boat, in the meantime, just kept on going.

One of the most comical—and dangerous—situations I've faced with a net resulted from a case of mistaken identity. As the tale unfolds, you'll bite your lip, but please reserve judgment until you read the conclusion. I'm an animal lover, too.

My friend, George Copeland, and I were at Raccoon Island at the mouth of Ft. Lauderdale's ancient New River, the one-time home of a trading post. We arrived via George's flats skiff, a 16-foot Chaparral that was built there in town, to net bait that we planned to use later on.

During the 1970's, I'd head south to fish Port Everglades and the surrounding area, where catching the live bait was tougher than the snook. We tried lighted helmets and dip nets on poles, whatever it took to accomplish our goal. In the end, however, we came back to cast nets.

George grew up nearby so he knew the waters. Still, we were sometimes forced to net for hours before fishing Pier 66 or the Coast Guard docks, where double-digit snook were the norm at that time. A 35-pounder that hangs in my office is a testament to what we caught.

George and I had gotten out of the skiff and headed off on the flat in different directions. I spotted what I thought was a school of "silvers" (our favorite variety) and started wading in their general direction. The folds of my 10-foot net were draped on shoulder, as I gripped the lead line between my teeth. All it would take, if I opened the net, would be a throw or two and we'd be set for the night.

Eventually, when I inched within range, I saw what appeared to be the school's outline. I twisted my torso, getting ready to throw.

After "pan-caking" the net and watching it land, I saw the eruption of foam. I figured I had netted the entire school, but then up pops the head of a manatee! It was completely encircled by the 20-foot spread.

With a massive swirl, the manatee took off, tightening the loop on my wrist. A second later, I was pulled off my feet and being dragged like an infant's pull-toy. Before I knew it, I was literally "on plane." I held my breath for as long as I could, while attempting to free my net hand. But try as I might, I couldn't do it. I considered at the time that I was a goner—the victim of what the ancients once thought were mermaids

Fear can double your strength when you need it. So I filled my lungs whenever I could, while gasping for breath by rolling over when I reached the surface. I was now hundreds of yards from shore, and tethered to the likes of a runaway train. For what it's worth, I was leaving a wake.

Don't ask me how, but at the last possible moment, the beast managed to break the draw strings. He was probably as relieved as I was, but now we were both literally in deep water. The first thing I managed to do was free my wrist, as I treaded water and scanned the horizon. Losing my cast net didn't matter; I was glad to be alive. I eventually heard George yelling in the distance. He had discovered that I was missing.

It took all my strength to swim back to shore. Shaking and sputtering, I was unable to speak until some time after George arrived on the scene. He probably doubted my story at first (who wouldn't), until he surveyed the damage. Not only was I bedraggled and spitting water, but my net was gone and my wrist, badly bruised.

It was hours later that I finally quit shivering and developed an interest in fishing again–with the few baits George had managed to net. He'd put several snook in the boat already (the limit was four apiece) in the neon glow of the Pier 66 sign.

What was perhaps my greatest cast net exploit involved something other than mullet. It all began at a local sports bar.

Try to visualize a Friday night, when the University of Miami Hurricanes were about to play Boston College. It was November 23, 1984. How can I remember such an obscure date? Well, it's when Doug Flutie threw that Hail Mary pass with only 24 seconds left on the clock, that won the game for Boston College. Miami, in the meantime, had just scored a touchdown, which all but assured their victory. Then, along comes Flutie in the final seconds. It was one of the greatest finishes in collegiate history.

I'd gone to the bar directly from work, I'm guessing around 6 p.m., to hang out and wait for the game to start. I had been there for 30 minutes when something rocked my world.

In through the door walked this vision in white, draped in a form-fitting dress. Her four-inch heels and tousled hair completed the total ensemble. For a moment, you could hear a pin drop.

In well-rehearsed fashion, she ordered a drink before carrying it to a stool at an empty bar, with no patrons or servers to create a distraction. Everyone stared before turning away, as the pre-game warm-up flashed on the TV screen. We all secretly ravished that beauty, who was sitting alone in the back. It took a few minutes to muster my courage.

I don't mind admitting that I'd had a few beers, or that I liked the company of beautiful women. So I grabbed my mug and made my move, to the amusement of everyone seated around me. "Is he nuts?" I heard someone mutter, as I pulled-up a stool beside her. The first thing I said, and it may sound corny, was "I'm here to protect you from all the animals."

To which she replied, after panning the room, "I only see one."

But she took the bait and told me her name, and later explained that she worked as a model. She was returning from an assignment in Ft. Lauderdale, and wanted to relax at the end of the day. Maybe we talked for 30 minutes, during which she said something about meeting people at a fancy night club that was located down the road. Apparently, it hadn't opened yet. Meanwhile, the Happy Hour crowd had started arriving in anticipation of the 9 p.m. game. When she stood-up to leave, every eye was on her—both male and female.

The game continued until after midnight, before ending with that last-minute pass: one of the greatest finishes ever recorded. Only two words can describe the bar at that time: Total pandemonium. Then suddenly the noise level dropped. She was back again and headed my way.

Only this time I was surrounded by my fishing buddies who'd come in to watch the game. When she whispered to the guy sitting next to me, "You're in my seat," he got up and moved. I didn't know it at first, but I'd hit the jackpot.

"I heard your friends talking about fishing. Are you a fisherman, too," she asked.

I nearly peed in my pants.

She then explained that she'd grown up in Lantana, and that she and her brother had fished the bridges for snook, with sand perch and mullet that they caught in a cast net. At that point my head started spinning.

All I could say was, "Baby, if you can tell me the first thing about cast nets, even how to hold one, I'll buy you a bottle of Dom Perignon."

At which time she explained how to fold the mesh, grip the lead line, things like that, and how she'd worn white rubber boots—like a commercial fisherman. By now, it was me who was trapped.

We drank that bottle and sat there till closing. Then we ended up dating and living together for a year or two, until I surprised her (and her date) at a fancy restaurant after, can you believe it, a football game!

We remained friends for a while after that, although we never did what we'd talked about–throwing a cast net from Lantana Bridge. That underscored what I said in the beginning: "A net only gives as good as it gets."

To order additional copies of
"A Net Full of Tails",
please go online to:
www.antiquereels.com/tgbooks